GCSE ENGLISH/ENGLISH L[

Extension Book

Richard Broomhead

Series Editor: Peter Buckroyd

SPECIFICATION A

OXFORD
UNIVERSITY PRESS

OXFORD
UNIVERSITY PRESS

Great Clarendon Street, Oxford OX2 6DP

Oxford University Press is a department of the University of Oxford.
It furthers the University's objective of excellence in research,
scholarship, and education by publishing worldwide in

Oxford New York

Auckland Bangkok Buenos Aires Cape Town Chennai
Dar es Salaam Delhi Hong Kong Istanbul Karachi Kolkata
Kuala Lumpur Madrid Melbourne Mexico City Mumbai Nairobi
São Paulo Shanghai Taipei Tokyo Toronto

Oxford is a registered trade mark of Oxford University Press
in the UK and in certain other countries

© Richard Broomhead 2003

British Library Cataloguing in Publication Data

Data available

ISBN 0 19 831899 5

10 9 8 7 6 5 4 3 2 1

Printed in Italy by Rotolito Lombarda

Acknowledgements

The Publisher would like to thank the following for permission to repro-
duce photographs:
BBC Picture Library: p 33; Bridgeman Art Library: pp 35, 59; Corel
Professional Photos: pp 16, 39, 46 (bottom), 48, 55, 65, 66, 86; Getty
Images/Photodisc: p 80; Heritage Picture Library: p 21, 84; Illustrated
London News: pp 13, 18, 19; NSPCC: p 44; PhotoAlto: p 79; Rex Features:
p 38; Royal Mail: 45; Keith Kent/Science Photo Library: title page; University
Library, Utrecht: p 22; Warwick Castle: p 46 (top);

Illustration (p 61) by Martin Ursell

Cover photographs by Keith Kent/Science Photo Library (background);
Hulton Archive (middle bottom); Illustrated London News (top).

We are grateful for permission to include the following copyright material
in this book:

Extract from *The New International Version of the Holy Bible* (NIV), copyright ©
International Bible Society, is reproduced by permission of the publishers,
Hodder & Stoughton Ltd. W H Auden: lines from 'Night Mail' from *W H
Auden: The Collected Poems* (1976), reprinted by permission of the publishers,
Faber & Faber Ltd. Gillian Clarke: 'No Hands' from *Collected Poems* (1997),
reprinted by permission of the publishers, Carcanet Press Ltd. Mike Coles:
extract from *The Bible in Cockney*, copyright © BRF 2001, reprinted by per-
mission of the Bible Reading Fellowship. Robert Crawshaw: 'Alright m8',
first published here by permission of the author. Richard Curtis and Ben
Elton: extract from 'Blackadder Goes Forth' in *Blackadder: The Whole Damn
Dynasty* (Michael Joseph, 1998), copyright © Richard Curtis and Ben Elton
1989, reprinted by permission of Penguin Books Ltd. Stephen Evans:
'September 11th' extract from *The Day That Shook the World* (BBC Books,
2001), reprinted by permission of BBC Worldwide Ltd. William Golding:
extract from *Lord of the Flies* (1954), reprinted by permission of the publishers, Faber & Faber Ltd. Seamus Heaney: lines from *Beowulf* (1999), reprinted
by permission of the publishers, Faber & Faber Ltd. Ted Hughes: lines from
'Tractor' from *Moortown Diary*, lines from 'Wind' from *Hawk in the Rain*, and
lines from 'Work and Play' from *Season Songs*, reprinted by permission of
the publishers, Faber & Faber Ltd. Brian Patten: extract from *Beowulf*
(Scholastic, 1999), copyright © Brian Patten 1999, reprinted by permission
of the author, c/o Rogers, Coleridge & White Ltd, 20 Powis Mews, London
W11 1JN. Annie Proulx: extract from *The Shipping News* (Fourth Estate,

1993), copyright © Annie Proulx 1993, reprinted by permission of
HarperCollins Publishers Ltd. Michèle Roberts: extract from *Flesh and Blood*
(Virago, 1995), copyright © Michèle Roberts 1995, reprinted by permission
of Time Warner Books UK. Delia Smith: 'Low-fat Moist Carrot Cake' from
Delia Smith's *How to Cook: Book One* (BBC, 1998), text copyright © Delia
Smith 1998, reprinted by permission of BBC Worldwide Ltd and Deborah
Owen Literary Agency on behalf of the author. John Steinbeck: extract
from *Of Mice and Men* (Penguin, 2000), copyright © John Steinbeck
1937,1965, reprinted by permission of Penguin Books Ltd. Rosemary
Sutcliffe: extract from *Beowulf: Dragonslayer* (Bodley Head, 1961), reprinted
by permission of the Random House Group Ltd.

and also to the following for their permission:

Amnesty International UK for extract from appeal leaflet. **BBC** for
extract from article 'Lunchtime quake shakes Manchester', BBC News
Online, 22.10.02. **Centrepoint** for extracts from a 1994 campaign leaflet.
The Independent for 'Spelt-Out' from *The Independent*, 4.9.02. **NI
Syndication** for 'Sca-a-a-ary but I like it' by Rachel Campbell-Johnston
from *The Times*, 7.10.00, copyright © NI Syndication Ltd, London 2000; and
'We're All Shook Up' by Lyndsey Weatherall and Jill Mowat from *The Sun*,
22.10.02, copyright © Lyndsey Weatherall and Jill Mowat/ News
International Newspapers Ltd, London 2002. **NSPCC** for poster from
national billboard campaign 2002. **Royal Mail** for advertisement for
British Philatelic Bureau. Anne Boleyn stamp copyright © Royal Mail 1997.
All rights reserved. **Warwick Castle** for advertisement 'Come face to face
with hand to hand'.

We regret we have been unable to trace and contact all copyright holders
of material included before publication. If notified the publisher under-
takes to rectify any errors or omissions at the earliest opportunity.

The extracts in this book are from the following recommended editions:
W.H. Auden, 'Night Mail' in *W.H. Auden: The Collected Poems*. London: Faber
and Faber, 1976 (edited by Edward Mendelson) **Jane Austen**, *Pride and
Prejudice*. Oxford World's Classics, OUP, 1998 **Rachael Bell**, *Queen Elizabeth I*.
Heinemann, 1998 **William Blake**, 'London' in *Selected Poetry of William
Blake*. Oxford: OUP, 1996 (with and introduction and notes by Michael
Mason) **William Blake**, 'The Sick Rose' in *William Blake: Selected Poetry*.
Oxford World's Classics, OUP, 1998 **Emily Brontë**, *Wuthering Heights*.
Oxford World's Classics, OUP, 1998 **Geoffrey Chaucer**, *The Riverside Chaucer
Third Edition*. OUP, 1988 **Gillian Clarke**, 'No Hands' in *Collected Poems*.
Carcanet Press, 1997 **Mike Coles**, *The Bible in Cockney*. The Bible Reading
Fellowship, 2001 **Michael Crichton**, *Jurassic Park*. Arrow, 1993 **Michael
Crichton**, *Travels*. Pan Books, 1988 **Curtis** & **Elton**, *Blackadder – The Whole
Damned Dynasty 1485 – 1917*. Penguin, 1999 **Terry Deary**, *Horrible Histories*:
'Elizabeth I - Frizzie Lizzie' from *Cruel Kings and Mean Queens*. Scholastic
Hippo, 1995 **Charles Dickens**, *Bleak House*. Oxford World's Classics, OUP,
1996 (edited and with an introduction by Stephen Gill) **Charles Dickens**,
Hard Times. Oxford World's Classics, OUP, 1998 **William Golding**, *Lord of
the Flies*. London: Faber and Faber, 1997 **Thomas Hardy**, *Far From the
Madding Crowd*. Oxford World's Classics, OUP, 2002 **Seamus Heaney**,
Beowulf. Faber and Faber, 2000 **Robert Herrick**, 'To the Virgins, To Make
Much of Time' in *Selected Poems of Robert Herrick*. Manchester: Carcanet New
Press, 1980 **Susan Hill**, *Mrs de Winter*. London: Compact Books, 1993 **Ted
Hughes**, 'Wind' and 'Thistles' in *New Selected Poems 1957 – 1994*. London:
Faber and Faber, 1995 **Ted Hughes**, 'Work and Play' and 'A Swallow' in
Season Songs. London: Faber and Faber, 1985 **Andrew Marvell**, 'To His Coy
Mistress' in *Complete Poems of Andrew Marvell*. Penguin, 1996 **The New
International Version of the Holy Bible**. Hodder and Stoughton
Religious, 1983 **Wilfred Owen**, 'Dulce Et Decorum Est' in *The Poems of
Wilfred Owen*. London: Chatto and Windus, 1990 (edited and with an intro-
duction by Jon Stallworthy OR The Penguin Book of First World War
Poetry. London: Penguin, 1985 (edited and with an introduction by Jon
Silkin) **The Paston Letters**, *A Selection in Modern Spelling*. Oxford World's
Classics, OUP, 1999 **Brian Patten**, *Beowulf*. Scholastic Hippo, 1999 **Sylvia
Plath**, 'Morning Song' in *Collected Poems*. London: Faber and Faber, 1981
Annie Proulx, *The Shipping News*. Fourth Estate (Harper Collins), 2002
Sir Walter Raleigh, 'What is our life?' in *Poems, Sir Walter Raleigh*. London:
Everyman, Phoenix, 1999 **Michèle Roberts**, *Flesh and Blood*. Virago Press,
1995 **William Shakespeare**, *Macbeth*. Oxford School Shakespeare, OUP,
2001 **William Shakespeare**, *Romeo and Juliet*. Oxford School Shakespeare,
OUP, 2001 **William Shakespeare**, 'Sonnet XII' in *The Complete Sonnets and
Poems*. Oxford World's Classics, OUP, 2002 **John Steinbeck**, *Of Mice and
Men*. London: Penguin, 2000 (with an introduction by Susan Shillinglaw)
Rosemary Sutcliffe, *Beowulf: Dragonslayer*. Bodley Head, 1961 **Neville
Williams**, *The Life and Times of Elizabeth I*. Doubleday, 1972

The information above was correct at the time of going to Press.

The publisher would like to thank the following consultants for their valu-
able advice on this book:
Dr Sandie Byrne, Fellow and Tutor in English, Balliol College, Oxford
Michele Paule, Senior Lecturer in Able/Gifted Education, Westminster
Institute of Education

The author would like to thank his Year 10 GCSE English group at
Debenham High School for trialling units and acting as 'guinea pigs', and
Robert Crawshaw for his help with text message language.

CONTENTS

INTRODUCTION

This *Extension Book* for AQA GCSE English and English Literature, Specification A, has been produced to help you reach the top grades in your coursework and examinations. It can be used in conjunction with any other core textbook – your teacher will help you to combine the material successfully – and can, itself, be used in a variety of ways, as shown in the diagram below.

As a teacher and GCSE examiner, I often come across bright students who are capable of high GCSE grades but fall short. This is often because they have not had enough practice at exploring key skills, including the nuances of language, style, structure, form, audience and context. Many students are able to spot techniques being used in texts but don't examine the effects of these or consider why a writer has used them. What are they trying to convey to you, the reader?

I have written this book with the aim of helping you to work on these skills and as a result, I hope, enable you to reach the top grades successfully.

Richard Broomhead
Suffolk 2003

POSSIBLE ROUTES THROUGH THE UNITS

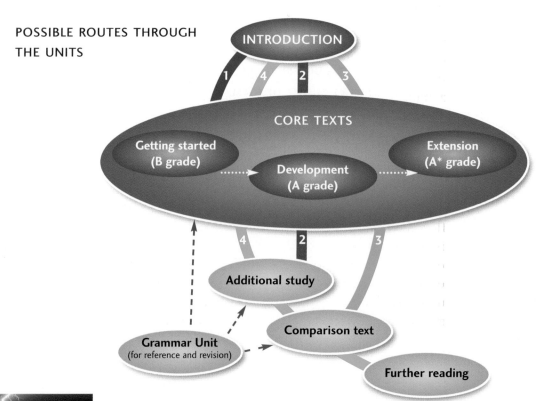

Route 1:
Introduction and Core texts

Route 2:
Introduction, Core texts and Additional study

Route 3:
Introduction, Core texts and Comparison text

Route 4:
Introduction, Core texts, Additional study, Comparison text and Further reading

1: Language for dramatic, poetic and figurative effect

Introduction

This section explores how language can be used to build up dramatic tension and to convey powerful images and emotions. You will analyze these techniques and consider the variety of effects that they can create.

Understanding the use of language for these effects will help you in both your coursework and the examinations. It is relevant to prose, poetry, drama and non-fiction texts.

Read this extract, in which a man is being pursued by a dinosaur:

> Stumbling over tree roots in the darkness, clawing his way past dripping branches, he saw the Jeep ahead, and the lights shining around the vertical wall of the barrier made him feel better. In a moment he'd be in the car and then he'd get the hell out of here. He scrambled around the barrier and then he froze.
>
> The animal was already there.

From *Jurassic Park* by Michael Crichton

Look at how the writer develops the drama. The words 'stumbling', 'clawing' and 'scrambled' convey a sense of panic and desperation, as the character attempts to escape from the dinosaur. The description of the setting builds up the drama: 'dripping', suggests that rain adds to the confusion, and 'darkness' increases the sense of menace.

The author's use of verb tenses also heightens the tension. 'Stumbling', 'clawing' and 'shining' are all present participles, which give a sense of immediacy. The change to the conditionals, 'he'd' (the contraction of 'he would'), reflect the fact that the character is looking forward to what he thinks is security, ahead. The tension is briefly relaxed. However, the next sentence ends with the word 'froze', which startles the reader as well as conveying the reaction of the character. The author follows up with a dramatic simple past tense sentence for effect: 'The animal was already there' and the drama is heightened once more.

Dramatic language – language that builds up an atmosphere of tension, suspense or drama

Look at the extract below, which describes a swallow flying about in summer.

> The swallow of summer, the seamstress of summer,
> She scissors the blue into shapes and she sews it

From 'Work and Play' by Ted Hughes

Hughes uses several poetic and figurative techniques to build up a vivid image:

◆ Alliteration. Hughes uses the repetition of 's' (sibilance) to create a rhythmical dragging effect that creates the idea of the bird flying. The alliteration also creates a sense of momentum in the metre to suggest the grace of the swallow (see page 90 for revision of metre).

◆ Metaphor. In his description of the swallow as 'the seamstress of summer', Hughes compares the swallow with someone who sews, suggesting that the bird helps to create the overall pattern of summer and draws it to him as a whole.

◆ The use of the word 'scissors' builds up the image of the swallow as a seamstress, and echoes the shape of the swallow's forked tail.

Poetic and figurative language – highly crafted language that conveys a powerful expression or emotion, often through imagery, careful choice of diction and in a highly structured pattern of stresses and rhythms. Such language often uses poetic techniques such as simile, metaphor, alliteration, assonance, onomatopoeia and motifs (distinctive themes or ideas that weave through a text).

CORE TEXT

The next passage is from Thomas Hardy's novel *Far from the Madding Crowd*. In this extract, Gabriel Oak and Bathsheba have been woken by a storm and try to cover the hayricks before it begins to rain.

A light flapped over the scene, as if reflected from phosphorescent wings crossing the sky, and a rumble filled the air. It was the first move of the approaching storm.

The second peal was noisy, with comparatively little visible lightning. Gabriel saw a candle shining in Bathsheba's bedroom, and soon a shadow swept to and fro upon the blind.

Then there came a third flash. Manoeuvres of a most extraordinary kind were going on in the vast firmamental hollows overhead. The lightning was now the colour of silver, and gleamed in the heavens like a mailed army. Rumbles became rattles. Gabriel from his elevated position could see over the landscape at least half-a-dozen miles in front. Every hedge, bush, and tree, was distinct as in a line engraving. In a paddock in the same direction was a herd of heifers, and the forms of these were visible at this moment in the act of galloping about in the wildest maddest confusion, flinging their heels and tails high into the air, their heads to earth. A poplar in the immediate foreground was like an ink stroke on burnished tin. Then the picture vanished, leaving the darkness so intense that Gabriel worked entirely by feeling with his hands . . .

. . . A blue light appeared in the zenith . . . It was the fourth of the larger flashes.

. . . Before Oak had laid his hands upon his tools again out leapt the fifth flash, with the spring of a serpent and the shout of a fiend. It was green as an emerald, and the reverberation was stunning . . . In the open ground before him, as he looked over the ridge of the rick, was a dark and apparently female form . . .

'Is that you, ma'am?' said Gabriel to the darkness.

'Who is there?' said the voice of Bathsheba.

'Gabriel. I am on the rick, thatching.'

. . . Heaven opened then indeed. The flash was almost too novel for its inexpressibly dangerous nature to be at once realised, and they could only comprehend the magnificence of its beauty. It sprang from east, west, north, south, and was a perfect dance of death. The forms of skeletons appeared in the air, shaped with blue fire for bones—dancing, leaping, striding, racing around, and mingling altogether in unparalleled confusion. With these were intertwined undulating snakes of green, and behind these was a broad mass of lesser light. Simultaneously came from every part of the tumbling sky what may be called a shout, since, though no shout ever came near it, it was more of the nature of a shout than of anything else earthly.

. . . Oak had hardly time to gather up these impressions into a thought . . . when the tall tree on the hill before-mentioned seemed on fire to a white heat, and a new one among these terrible voices mingled with the last crash of those preceding. It was a stupifying blast, harsh and pitiless, and it fell upon their ears in a dead, flat blow, without that reverberation which leads the tones of a drum to more distant thunder. By the lustre reflected from every part of the earth . . . he saw that the tree was sliced down the whole length of its tall straight stem, a huge riband of bark being apparently flung off . . . The lightning had struck the tree. A sulphurous smell filled the air: then all was silent, and black as a cave in Hinnom.

From Far from the Madding Crowd by Thomas Hardy

ACTIVITIES *Getting started*

1 Hardy uses several figurative and poetic techniques to bring the scene to life. Look at the techniques below and match them up to the correct example.

Technique	Example
Personification	Flapped, flash, rumbles
Simile	. . . out leapt the fifth flash, with the spring of a serpent . . .
Metaphor	Every hedge, bush, and tree, was distinct as in a line engraving.
Onomatopoeia	With these were intertwined undulating snakes of green . . .

2 Look back at your answers in question 1. For each example of technique, write a short explanation of the effect that it creates.

3 How does Hardy build up the developing drama in the scene? Look at his use of discourse connectives. (See page 96 for revision of discourse connectives).

Development

ACTIVITIES 4 In question 1, you looked at figurative techniques that Hardy uses in the passage. Find another example of each technique and examine what effects you think they create. Copy and complete a grid like the one below.

Technique	Example	Effects
Personification		
Simile		
Metaphor		
Onomatopoeia		

5 One way in which Hardy controls the drama is through his use of sentence types. Reread paragraph 3 of the extract, then write a short explanation of how Hardy varies his sentence types to create dramatic effects. (See page 95 for revision of sentence types.)

Extension

ACTIVITIES 6 The scene is chaotic and dramatic. How does Hardy create drama in the passage? Write an extended paragraph focusing on:

- the use of verbs to reveal the chaos and evoke a sense of unleashed energy
- the use of colour and references to light
- how Hardy makes the scene almost supernatural
- how he gives the storm character
- any other ideas of your own.

7 Although this is a piece of prose, it is very poetic in places. Select two examples where you feel Hardy's style is poetic and explain what effects these create in the passage.

ADDITIONAL STUDY

ACTIVITY Use the Hardy passage to produce a tabloid newspaper report in which you dramatize and over-exaggerate the storm. In your writing, think about:

- the features of tabloid newspapers, such as dramatic headlines, topic sentences, emotive and extended noun phrases, colourful adjectives to dramatize the event, bias and opinion, simple language, quotations and interviews
- the use of figurative language to bring the scene to life for the reader
- the use of dramatic and active verbs to convey the chaos of the scene.

COMPARISON TEXT

ACTIVITY Read the extract (on page 10) from the travel supplement of *The Times*. The writer describes her experience on a roller coaster ride.

Examine how both writers (Hardy and Campbell-Johnston) build up a picture of the scene in their writing. Think about:

- how each writer uses figurative and poetic language and the effects created
- how each writer builds up the drama of the scene and the effects created
- how sentence types and structures control the drama of the scene
- which writer uses language most effectively, in your opinion, and why.

'That's the sc-a-a-a-riest seat,' he told me. And he managed to put so much fear into that one protracted vowel that I would have leapt from my place right there and then if a security man hadn't come round just at that moment and locked me tightly back in with a metal safety bar. There was no escape now. I was in for the ride.

And not just any ride. This was Blackpool's star-billed Big One: 'the tallest, fastest and most sensational roller coaster in the world'. It climbs to a height of 235 feet before hurling itself down structures of iron at nerve-stripping speeds of up to 85 miles per hour.

And, clearly the man behind me wasn't going to be any help. 'You are about to experience the ride of your life,' he yelped into my earhole – just as the Tannoy informed me of the very same thing. And then the roller coaster was off, trundling away from its platform, with me, like an egg in a carton, in the very front seat.

Tchika, tchika, tchika... a chain ratcheted the line of little carriages higher and higher up a slope. Far beneath, the fairground gradually receded. I could see the whole of the Pleasure Beach spread out below, its merry-go-rounds no bigger than musical boxes, its coaster tracks like Meccano toys and the frills of water that ruffled out around the log *flume looked as still as waves when you watch them from an aeroplane window... Oh my God! Had I got as high as that?

The man in the carriage behind me was ominously quiet. And then the train reached the pinnacle. I could feel it crawling over the hump and could see the grey of the Irish Sea spreading way out ahead of me. I was over the highest part, beginning to descend... but still nothing, nothing, it seemed, was going to happen. For a moment I almost dared to breath with relief.

And then the horizon just vanished.

I was in free fall. I was hurtling through space. And there was no way that the safety bar was going to hold me, there was no way the train was going to stay on its rail. Was that my life spinning somewhere inside me? Were those images of my childhood flashing up before my eyes? Would I faint? Oh my God, what if I was going to faint? The wind ripped my shrieking from between deadlocked jaws.

And from then I remember nothing but swooping and plunging, the terror of horizons being sliced away at one side, the swerves and the sidekicks, the veer and the lunge, until at last, when I thought I could take it no longer, when I thought that white knuckles could no longer grip, I was hurtling through a tunnel and the train was gradually slowing, it was drawing back towards the platform and coming to a stop.

My skull felt wobbly on its stalk by the time I got out.

'Scareeeeee, eh, lass?' was all that the man in the seat behind me could contribute. Nobody else spoke. They were grinning and giggling, their throats dry with wind.

And that was it – my first ride on the Pepsi Max Big One.

Rachel Campbell-Johnston – *The Times*, Saturday 7 October 2000

* flume – an artificial, sloping channel, through which water flows

FURTHER READING

Gillian Clarke, 'The Field-Mouse' (*Fivefields*, Carcanet Press, 1998). Reprinted in AQA *Anthology* Specification A

Ted Hughes, 'Tractor' and 'Wind' in *New Selected Poems 1957–1994* (Faber and Faber, 1995), 'Work and Play' in *Season Songs* (Faber and Faber, 1985)

Laurie Lee, *Cider with Rosie* (Penguin, 1998)

William Shakespeare, many plays but in particular *Romeo and Juliet* (Oxford School Shakespeare, OUP, 2001), *Macbeth* (Oxford School Shakespeare, OUP, 2001), *A Midsummer Night's Dream* (Oxford School Shakespeare, OUP, 2001)

2. Language for ironic and emotive effect

Introduction

This section explores how language can be used to affect a reader's emotions or be used to create a sarcastic effect and make the audience think. You will develop your ability to analyze these techniques and comment on them in your writing.

Look at these extracts:

> 'It is a truth universally acknowledged, that a single man in possession of a good fortune, must be in want of a wife.'

From *Pride and Prejudice* by Jane Austen

Austen is being ironic – firstly, no 'truth' is ever 'universally acknowledged', and secondly in her times, *women* were desperate to marry a rich man and find security. The single, rich *men* did not necessarily share the same desperation. Austen means the opposite of what she writes.

KEY TERM

Irony – where language or expression are used in opposition to the meaning. Sarcasm is a type of irony, used for mockery.

> In 1999 we recorded torture cases in 132 countries. We believe the real statistics to be much higher.
>
> Take the case of 24 year old Nang Mai. Nang was seized by soldiers in June 1997 in her township in Myanmar – not for any particular offence, but simply for belonging to an ethnic minority. She was repeatedly raped, covered with wood and burnt alive.

From an Amnesty International leaflet

Here the language is heavily emotive to get us interested in the work of Amnesty International. For example:

◆ a statistic is used (132) to shock us, but then Amnesty follow this up by saying that they think 'the real statistics to be much higher', which increases the reader's sense of shock
◆ to add to the emotive effects, a person is named to make them real to the reader (more than a statistic)

- ◆ the verb 'seized' suggests pain and suffering
- ◆ the writer ends with a shocking and highly emotive pattern of three: 'repeatedly raped, covered with wood and burnt alive'. This builds up the image of suffering. The adverb 'repeatedly' adds impact, while 'alive' conveys the horror of the situation.

KEY
🔒 TERM

Emotive language – language that appeals to our emotions and feelings (usually to provoke a specific reaction)

CORE TEXTS

Look at the text below. It is an extract of script from the television series *Blackadder Goes Forth* and it is set just before the end of the First World War. George, a simpleton, is discussing his friends, who have died during the war, with Blackadder. This is from the final episode of the series, in which all the characters die.

Blackadder	Oh, for God's sake, George, how long have you been in the army?
George	What, me? Oh, I joined up straight away – 10 August 1914. What a day that was. Myself and the fellows leap-frogging down to Cambridge recruiting office, then playing tiddly-winks in the queue. We'd hammered the hell out of Oxford's tiddly-winkers only the week before and here we were off to hammer the Boche. A crashingly superb bunch of blokes, fine, clean-limbed – even our acne had a strange nobility about it.
Blackadder	Yes, and how are your boys now?
George	Well, Jocko and the Badger bought it at the first Ypres, unfortunately – quite a shock that. I remember Bumfluff's house-master wrote and told me that Sticky had been out for a duck and the Gubber had snitched a parcel sausage end and gone goose-over-stumps frog-side.
Blackadder	Meaning?
George	I don't know, sir, but I read in *The Times* that they'd both been killed.
Blackadder	And Bumfluff himself?
George	Copped a packet at Gallipoli with the Ozzies. So did Drippy and Strangely Brown – I remember we heard it on the first morning of the Somme when Titch and Mr Floppy got gassed back to Blighty.
Blackadder	Which leaves?
George	Gosh, yes – I suppose I'm the only one of the Trinity's Tiddlers still alive. Cor blimey – there's a thought, and not a jolly one.

ACTIVITY Working in pairs, explore how the *Blackadder* passage is both emotive and ironic.

Now look at the following poem, written by Wilfred Owen, who fought and died in the First World War. The poem was seen as an anti-war text during its time as Owen is blunt about the horrors and reality of life on the front line.

Dulce Et Decorum Est

Bent double, like old beggars under sacks,   1
Knock-kneed, coughing like hags, we cursed through sludge,
Till on the haunting flares we turned our backs
And towards our distant rest began to trudge.
Men marched asleep. Many had lost their boots   5
But limped on, blood-shod. All went lame; all blind;
Drunk with fatigue; deaf even to the hoots
Of tired, outstripped Five-Nines that dropped behind.
Gas! Gas! Quick, boys! – An ecstasy of fumbling,
Fitting the clumsy helmets just in time;   10
But someone still was yelling out and stumbling,
And flound'ring like a man in fire or lime. . .
Dim, through the misty panes and thick green light,
As under a green sea, I saw him drowning.

In all my dreams, before my helpless sight,   15
He plunges at me, guttering, choking, drowning.
If in some smothering dreams you too could pace
Behind the wagon that we flung him in,
And watch the white eyes writhing in his face,
His hanging face, like a devil's sick of sin;   20
If you could hear, at every jolt, the blood
Come gargling from the froth-corrupted lungs,
Obscene as cancer, bitter as the cud
Of vile, incurable sores on innocent tongues,
My friend, you would not tell with such high zest   25
To children ardent for some desperate glory,
The old Lie; Dulce et Decorum est
Pro patria mori.

Getting started

1 Look at these verbs from the poem:
    ◆ bent   ◆ cursed   ◆ coughing   ◆ trudged.

    What do you notice about the verbs? Find three more examples of verbs that are used emotively in Owen's poem and explain how effective you find them.

2 In line 16, Owen uses an emotive pattern of three verbs. Find these and write them down, then answer these questions:
    Why do you think he chose to use three verbs?
    Why do you think Owen chose these specific verbs?
    What effect do they create?

3 Find the pronoun that Owen uses to approach his reader directly. How effective do you think this is and why?

Development

4 As the poem progresses, Owen refers to 'Men' (line 5); 'boys' (line 9); 'children' (line 26). Why do you think he chooses these words in this order?

5 Owen uses an ironic euphemism in line 4: 'towards our distant rest began to trudge'. Explain in a few sentences why he might have used this, and how effective you find it.

K E Y
TERM

Euphemism – when a mild or concealing expression is substituted for a blunt or harsh one

6 Owen uses several emotive images in the poem, for example: 'an ecstacy of fumbling'. Think about why he uses this phrase and how the language can be read ironically and emotively. Find one more example and explore how well you think it works.

Extension

7 The poem's title and ending come from Latin and roughly mean 'It is good and honourable to die for one's country'. Why do you think Owen wrote this in Latin when it carries the main message of the poem?

8 This poem was published before Owen died, but the authorities were unhappy about people reading it (especially potential new recruits). What do you think makes the poem so powerful? Think about:
    ◆ why the poem is written as two 14-line sonnets (a form often used to express intense feelings of love and desire)

- ◆ why the poet uses a controlled rhyme scheme
- ◆ the use of iambic pentameter (10 beats per line) and why this occasionally breaks for effect.

How successful do you think Owen is in conveying his point of view?

ADDITIONAL STUDY

ACTIVITY Prepare a speech, aimed at people your own age, to persuade them that war is wrong. Use ideas and techniques from the poem such as:

- ◆ pattern of three ideas
- ◆ emotive language
- ◆ ironic language
- ◆ direct approach to the listener
- ◆ the use of figurative language and images
- ◆ points developed in sequence building an emotional crescendo to a climax at the end.

To reach the highest grades, you need to:

- ◆ structure your ideas clearly and logically
- ◆ engage your listener and be persuasive
- ◆ use dynamic and influential language
- ◆ make powerful and thought-provoking points.

Deliver your speech to the class. You may want to use ICT and deliver your speech and analysis as a PowerPoint presentation. Your teacher might use this as part of your coursework for Speaking and Listening as an Individual Extended Contribution. As an extension, you might want to write a short analysis of how your speech was received, and comment on the techniques you used and the intended effect. This sort of analysis will help you reach the top GCSE grades and move towards A level.

COMPARISON TEXT

This text (on page 16) was originally published by the charity, Centrepoint, to make the public more aware of homelessness and to encourage donations.

Although you will not be asked to compare a poem with a piece of media, the following activity is good preparation for Paper 1 of the English exam where you will be expected to compare at least two texts.

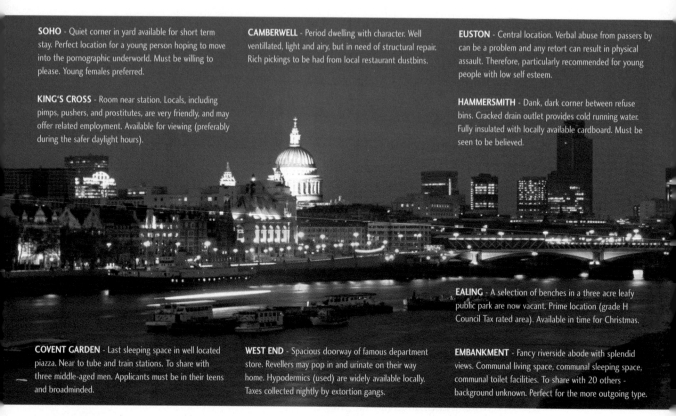

SOHO - Quiet corner in yard available for short term stay. Perfect location for a young person hoping to move into the pornographic underworld. Must be willing to please. Young females preferred.

KING'S CROSS - Room near station. Locals, including pimps, pushers, and prostitutes, are very friendly, and may offer related employment. Available for viewing (preferably during the safer daylight hours).

CAMBERWELL - Period dwelling with character. Well ventillated, light and airy, but in need of structural repair. Rich pickings to be had from local restaurant dustbins.

EUSTON - Central location. Verbal abuse from passers by can be a problem and any retort can result in physical assault. Therefore, particularly recommended for young people with low self esteem.

HAMMERSMITH - Dank, dark corner between refuse bins. Cracked drain outlet provides cold running water. Fully insulated with locally available cardboard. Must be seen to be believed.

EALING - A selection of benches in a three acre leafy public park are now vacant. Prime location (grade H Council Tax rated area). Available in time for Christmas.

COVENT GARDEN - Last sleeping space in well located piazza. Near to tube and train stations. To share with three middle-aged men. Applicants must be in their teens and broadminded.

WEST END - Spacious doorway of famous department store. Revellers may pop in and urinate on their way home. Hypodermics (used) are widely available locally. Taxes collected nightly by extortion gangs.

EMBANKMENT - Fancy riverside abode with splendid views. Communal living space, communal sleeping space, communal toilet facilities. To share with 20 others - background unknown. Perfect for the more outgoing type.

ACTIVITY Analyze and comment on the effectiveness of the linguistic techniques used in 'Dulce Et Decorum Est' and the Centrepoint leaflet. Think about:

- how language is used for emotive effect by each writer
- how language is employed for ironic effect in each text
- which text you think is the more successful.

To reach the highest grades you need to:

- show understanding when analyzing the techniques used
- support your ideas with detailed reference to the texts
- consider alternative interpretations and make cross references
- refer in detail to the structure, language and effects of the texts.

FURTHER READING

Jane Austen, *Emma* (Oxford World's Classics, OUP, 1998)

Jane Austen, *Pride and Prejudice* (Oxford World's Classics, OUP, 1998)

Richard Curtis and Ben Elton, *Blackadder - The Whole Damned Dynasty 1485-1917* (Penguin, 1999)

Jonathan Swift, *A Modest Proposal* (Oxford World's Classics, *Swift: Major Works*, OUP, 1998)

3: Patterns and details of words and images

Introduction

Writers use language in diverse ways to achieve effects. One way is to use patterned language, such as repetition of words or structures, to reinforce a point or to give cohesion to a text. Writers build up detail using devices such as noun phrases, imagery, sensory language, symbolism and atmospherics. In this section, you will study how writers achieve effects through their use of these linguistic techniques.

CORE TEXTS

Patterns and details of words

Look at the extract below. It is from a speech delivered at a Women's Rights convention in 1851.

> Dat man ober dar say dat womin needs to be helped into carriages, and lifted over ditches, and to hab de best place everywhar. Nobody eber helps me into carriages, or ober mud-puddles, or gibs me any best place. And a'n't I a woman? Look at me! Look at my arm! I have ploughed and planted, and gathered into barns, and no man could head me! And a'n't I a woman? I could work as much and eat as much as a man – when I could get it – and bear de lash as well! And a'n't I a woman? I have borne thirteen children, and see 'em mos' all sold off to slavery, and when I cried out with my mother's grief, none but Jesus heard me! And a'n't I a woman?

A black American slave, Sojourner Truth, 1851

Notice how patterns and details of words are used to make the speech effective. Truth uses a repeated pattern of rhetorical questions, 'And a'n't I a woman?', to draw attention to the injustice suffered by black women. The repetition gives the argument force and momentum. It also fixes the question firmly in the listeners' mind.

Truth repeats the imperative, 'Look', to command her listeners' attention. Then she goes on to use a pattern of three ideas to show how harshly she is treated: 'I have ploughed and planted, and gathered into barns . . . I could work as much and eat as much as a man ... and bear de lash as well!' She opens the speech with a pattern of three ideas (three 'needs' of a white woman) and then goes on to refute this to make her argument valid and clear.

Images

The following extract is from a poem about the birth of a child.

> Love set you going like a fat gold watch

From 'Morning Song' by Sylvia Plath

This is a highly effective image as it works on several levels. There are many valid interpretations and connotations. The simile implies that the child is precious (like 'gold') and is 'fat', suggesting that it is valuable and bursting with health. The word 'fat' also evokes an image of the mother's body, swollen as the child grows in her womb. The parents' love for each other is evident in that the child is compared with something of great value, implying that he/she is wanted. In addition, the ticking of a 'watch' echoes the child's heart beat.

CORE TEXT

The following extract describes a fictional town, Coketown.

It was a town of red brick, or of brick that would have been red if the smoke and ashes had allowed it; but as matters stood it was a town of unnatural red and black like the painted face of a savage. It was a town of machinery and tall chimneys, out of which interminable serpents of smoke trailed themselves for ever and ever, and never got uncoiled. It had a black canal in it, and a river that ran purple with ill-smelling dye, and vast piles of buildings full of windows where there was a rattling and a trembling all day long, and where the piston of the steam-engine worked monotonously up and down like the head of an elephant in a state of melancholy madness. It contained several large streets all very like one another, and many small streets still more like one another, inhabited by people equally like one another, who all went in and out at the same hours, with the same sound upon the same pavements, to do the same work, and to whom every day was the same as yesterday and to-morrow, and every year the counterpart of the last and the next.

These attributes of Coketown were in the main inseparable from the work by which it was sustained; against them were to be set off, comforts of life which found their way all over the world, and elegancies of life which, we will not ask how much of made the fine lady, who could scarcely bear to hear the place mentioned. The rest of its features were voluntary, and they were these.

You saw nothing in Coketown but what was severely workful. If the members of a religious persuasion built a chapel there—as the members of eighteen religious persuasions had done—they made it a pious warehouse of red brick, with sometimes (but this is only in highly ornamental examples) a bell in a birdcage on the top of it. The solitary exception was the New Church; a stuccoed edifice with a square steeple over the door, terminating in four short pinnacles like florid wooden legs. All the public inscriptions in the town were painted alike, in severe characters of black and white. The jail might have been the infirmary, the infirmary might have been the jail, the town-hall might have been either, or both, or anything else, for anything that appeared to the contrary in the graces of their construction. Fact, fact, fact, everywhere in the material aspect of the town; fact, fact, fact, everywhere in the immaterial.

From *Hard Times* by Charles Dickens

Getting started

ACTIVITIES

1 Dickens writes in detail to present the reader with a vivid image of Coketown. One way in which he does this is through his use of noun phrases. Look at these examples from the passage:

> 'a river that ran purple with *ill-smelling dye*'
> '*vast piles* of buildings'

Explain how these noun phrases help the reader to visualize the setting and what impression they convey of the place.

2 Another technique that Dickens uses to develop the setting is through imagery. Look at these examples from the passage:

> 'it was a town of unnatural red and black like the painted face of a savage'
>
> 'interminable serpents of smoke trailed themselves'
>
> 'the piston of the steam-engine worked monotonously up and down like the head of an elephant in a state of melancholy madness'

For each example, explain which figurative technique is being used and comment on how effective it is.

Development

ACTIVITIES

3 To build up detail in his writing, Dickens uses both colourful imagery and symbolic colour (where the colours have a significance beyond their visual impact, for example associations of mood or quality). Write a list of the colours that Dickens mentions in the passage. Why do you think he uses these colours? What effect do they convey?

4 Re-read the first paragraph. It is made up of four sentences.
   ◆ Look at how each one begins and explain why Dickens uses this patterned technique. What effect might he be aiming to create?
   ◆ Why do you think Dickens chose to use such long, complex sentences?

Extension

ACTIVITIES

5 In the first and final paragraphs, Dickens uses repetition and patterns of language for effect. Find two examples where he does this and consider the effects created.

6 In this passage, Dickens uses contrasts within sentences. Find an example in the final paragraph and analyze what effects are created.

7 Dickens conveys Coketown as an unpleasant and oppressive setting. What techniques does he use to make this apparent? Think about:

- sentence structures
- contrast within sentences
- colour symbolism
- patterns and repetition
- images
- noun phrases.

Additional study

ACTIVITY

In Paper 2 of the English examination, you will be asked to complete a piece of writing to 'inform, explain or describe'. In the activity below, you will focus on writing to describe, employing the techniques that you have learned about from work on the Dickens passage.

Write a descriptive account of a place that you dislike. This might be:

- a holiday location
- where you live
- school.

In your writing, use techniques that make your dislike clear (as Dickens did), so remember to think about:

- sentence structures for effect
- repetition
- colour symbolism
- imagery
- noun phrases
- patterns of language
- contrast within sentences
- variety of vocabulary and syntax (the arrangement of words and phrases).

Comparison text

ACTIVITY

Read the poem on page 21. It was written in the eighteenth century and explores how the city of London became an unpleasant and degrading place.

Compare how Dickens and Blake reveal their dislike of the setting through their use of linguistic techniques. Think about:

- patterns of language
- repetition
- contrasts used for effect
- sentence structures used for effect
- imagery and details of words
- colour symbolism used for effect.

London

by William Blake

I wander through each *chartered street,
Near where the chartered Thames does flow,
And mark in every face I meet
Marks of weakness, marks of woe.

In every cry of every man,
In every infant's cry of fear,
In every voice, in every ban,
The mind-forged manacles I hear:

How the chimney-sweeper's cry
Every black'ning church appalls;
And the hapless soldier's sigh
Runs in blood down palace walls.

But most through midnight streets I hear
How the youthful harlot's curse
Blasts the new-born infant's tear,
And blights with plagues the marriage hearse.

> * **chartered** – charters were originally given to cities as a sign of their freedom and liberty. However, Blake uses the term ironically, because in his time, many people regarded these charters as oppressive, denying citizens the basic rights they were designed to guarantee.

FURTHER READING

John Agard, 'Half-Caste', from *Get Back Pimple* (Penguin, 1996), reprinted in the AQA *Anthology* Specification A

W. H. Auden, 'Night Mail' in *Collected Poems of W.H. Auden* (Faber and Faber, 1976) Ted Hughes, 'The Warm and the Cold' in *New Selected Poems 1957 – 1994* (Faber and Faber, 1995)

Dylan Thomas, 'Do Not Go Gentle Into That Good Night' in *Collected Poems of Dylan Thomas 1934 – 1953* (Phoenix, 2000)

C. Tichborne 'Tichborne's Elegy', reprinted in the AQA *Anthology* Specification A

4: LAYERS OF MEANING IN LANGUAGE, IDEAS AND THEMES

INTRODUCTION

Many texts work on different levels. For example, fairy tales were originally told as allegories to warn young people against the dangers of being led astray: wolves and witches represented evil; grandparents and young children represented vulnerability; forests and lonely cottages represented seclusion and isolation. Think of a story you have read that works on more than one level.

Read the poem below.

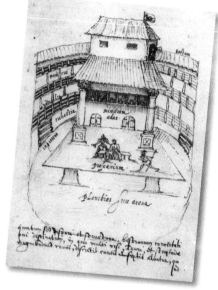

What is our life?

by Sir Walter Raleigh

What is our life? A play of passion.
And what our mirth but music of division?
Our mothers' wombs the tiring houses be
Where we are dressed for this short comedy.
Heaven the judicious sharp spectator is
Who sits and marks what here we do amiss.
The graves that hide us from the searching sun
Are like drawn curtains when the play is done.
Thus playing post we to our latest rest,
And then we die in earnest, not in jest.

This poem is an extended metaphor that compares life to a theatrical performance. The theatrical performance is one layer of description, the course of life and death is the deeper meaning. Notice how Raleigh compares pregnancy (in 'mothers' wombs') to getting ready for a performance in the dressing room ('tiring houses'). He goes on to compare life to a 'short comedy', with God ('Heaven') as the audience watching the performance. He compares death to the end of a performance, when the curtains are drawn.

KEY TERM

Extended metaphor – a metaphor that recurs through a passage of text or poem, building and expanding an image for comparison. An extended metaphor can run through a whole story. For example, *Animal Farm* by George Orwell is about animals rebelling against the tyrannical regime of Farmer Jones and humans, but it is also an extended metaphor about the Russian Revolution, in which Tsar Nicholas II was removed from power by the Bolsheviks.

CORE TEXTS

The Sick Rose
by William Blake

O rose, thou art sick;
The invisible worm
That flies in the night,
In the howling storm,

Has found out thy bed
Of crimson joy,
And his dark secret love
Does thy life destroy.

ACTIVITY

In a small group, discuss the possible layers of meaning in the poem. Read the interpretations below and decide which ones you find most valid. Be prepared to explain your views to others in the class.

- The poem is about a rose being eaten by a worm and decaying.
- It is a poem exploring the loss of sexual innocence in a female.
- The poem is a political metaphor about power and how it can be abused and corrupted.
- The poem is about life and death.
- The poem is about the loss of religion and how evil can intrude and destroy life.

There are other interpretations that can be developed. Think of alternative layers of meaning and be prepared to justify your thoughts.

Read the extract below from *Lord of the Flies* by William Golding.

Within the diamond haze of the beach something dark was fumbling along. Ralph saw it first, and watched till the intentness of his gaze drew all eyes that way. Then the creature stepped from mirage on to clear sand, and they saw that the darkness was not all shadow but mostly clothing. The creature was a party of boys, marching approximately in step in two parallel lines and dressed in strangely eccentric clothing. Shorts, shirts, and different garments they carried in their hands: but each boy wore a square black cap with a silver badge in it. Their bodies, from throat to ankle, were hidden by black cloaks which bore a long silver cross on the left breast and each neck was finished off with a hambone frill. The heat of the tropics, the descent, the search for food, and now this sweaty march along the blazing beach had given them the complexions of newly washed plums. The boy who controlled them was dressed in the same way though his cap badge was golden. When his party was about ten yards from the platform he shouted an order and they halted, gasping, sweating, swaying in the fierce light. The boy himself came forward, vaulted on to the platform with his cloak flying, and peered into what to him was almost complete darkness.

'Where's the man with the trumpet?'

Ralph, sensing his sun-blindness, answered him.

'There's no man with a trumpet. Only me.'

The boy came close and peered down at Ralph, screwing up his face as he did so. What he saw of the fair-haired boy with the creamy shell on his knees did not seem to satisfy him. He turned quickly, his black cloak circling.

'Isn't there a ship, then?'

Inside the floating cloak he was tall, thin, and bony: and his hair was red beneath the black cap. His face was crumpled and freckled, and ugly without silliness. Out of this face stared two light blue eyes, frustrated now, and turning, or ready to turn, to anger.

'Isn't there a man here?'

Ralph spoke to his back.

'No we're having a meeting. Come and join in.'

The group of cloaked boys began to scatter from close line. The tall boy shouted at them.

'Choir! Stand still!'

Wearily obedient, the choir huddled into line and stood there swaying in the sun. None the less, some began to protest faintly.

'But, Merridew. Please, Merridew… can't we?'

Then one of the boys flopped on his face in the sand and the line broke up. They heaved the fallen boy to the platform and let him lie. Merridew, his eyes staring, made the best of a bad job.

'All right then. Sit down. Let him alone.'

'But Merridew.'

'He's always throwing a faint,' said Merridew. 'He did in Gib.; and Addis; and at *matins over the *precentor.'

This last piece of shop brought sniggers from the choir, who perched like black birds on the criss-cross trunks and examined Ralph with interest. Piggy asked no names. He was intimidated by this uniformed superiority and the offhand authority in Merridew's voice.

* matins – morning prayer
  precentor – person who leads the singing in church services

From *Lord of the Flies* by William Golding

Getting started

ACTIVITIES

1 Read the first paragraph and list all the references to light and colour. What do these all have in common?

2 Most of the references to light and colour in the first paragraph are related to Jack ('Merridew') and the choir. What do these references suggest about the characters, even before they speak in the text?

Development

ACTIVITIES

3 Look at the end of the first paragraph (from 'The boy who controlled them…') and list all the verbs that relate to how the boy behaves. What do these suggest about his character?

4 Golding describes Jack as:

'. . . tall, thin, and bony: and his hair was red beneath the black cap. His face was crumpled and freckled, and ugly without silliness. Out of this face stared two light blue eyes, frustrated now, and turning, or ready to turn, to anger.'

What does this physical description suggest about Jack as a person?

Extension

ACTIVITIES

5 Golding says that the choir 'perched like black birds on the criss-cross trunks'. What could this imply about the choir and its role later in the novel?

6 *Lord of the Flies* was written shortly after the Second World War. Critics have suggested that the novel is a political allegory based on this event. The novel is centred on a deserted island. Based on your reading of this passage, who do you think Jack and the choir might represent? Give evidence to support your views.

ADDITIONAL STUDY

ACTIVITY

This task could count towards part of your coursework for Original Writing.

Write a short story that can be read on several levels. For example, it could be understood on one level by a child but on another level by an adult (think back to the fairy tales mentioned in the Introduction). Consider using:

◆ colour symbolism
◆ symbols

◆ characteristics that might mean more than one thing
◆ imagery that works on several levels.

Once you have written your story, produce a short explanation outlining how it works on several levels. You could present your story and explanation to the class as part of your Speaking and Listening coursework.

COMPARISON TEXT

ACTIVITY   Read the poem 'The Field-Mouse' by Gillian Clarke (reprinted in AQA *Anthology* Specification A).

Analyze how the *Lord of the Flies* extract and 'The Field-Mouse' can be read on a variety of levels, commenting on why each writer uses this layering technique.

FURTHER READING

John Agard, 'Half-Caste' (AQA *Anthology* Specification A)

William Blake, *Songs of Innocence and Experience* (Oxford World's Classics, OUP, 1998)

Gillian Clarke, 'The Field-Mouse'; 'On the Train' (AQA *Anthology* Specification A)

William Shakespeare, *As You Like It* Act 2 Scene 7, Jaques' speech 'all the world's a stage . . .' (Oxford School Shakespeare, OUP, 2002); *Henry V* Act 1 Scene 1, the Bishop of Ely's speech about strawberries (Oxford School Shakespeare, OUP, 2001); *Richard II* Act 3 Scene 4, the conversation between the gardener and servants (Oxford School Shakespeare, OUP, 1998)

5: WRITER'S NARRATIVE CRAFT AND VOICE

INTRODUCTION

Writers use different narrative devices and techniques to recount events. Some writers use a narrative style that is descriptive, aiming to develop a clear, flowing picture in the reader's mind; others use a more fact-packed, fast-paced style of narrative, which has less description but more action.

Every narrative has a 'voice'. It can be the voice of one or more characters, within the story, who tell the reader what has happened. This 'voice' is written in the first person. Alternatively, it can be the voice of someone outside the story.

This section focuses on different narrative styles adopted by writers for different effects.

Narrative craft
Read the extract below.

> The undertaker's men were like crows, stiff and black, and the cars were black, lined up beside the path that led to the church; and we, we too were black, as we stood in our pathetic, awkward group waiting for them to lift out the coffin and shoulder it, and for the clergyman to arrange himself; and he was another black crow, in his long cloak.
>
> And then the real crows rose suddenly from the trees and from the fields, whirled up like scraps of blackened paper from a bonfire, and circled, caw-caw-ing above our heads.

From *Mrs de Winter* by Susan Hill

Hill uses several narrative devices to engage the reader and to convey a strong impression of the setting and mood. The narrative style is full of imagery. Look at the simile: 'The undertaker's men were like crows'. This creates an image of men wearing long black coats, and suggests that they are like carrion birds around a carcass. The repetition of the word 'black' creates an atmosphere of gloom and misery. It is a word often associated with death, sorrow, unhappiness and evil. Hill adds sound to the scene by using onomatopoeia to describe the real crows: 'caw-caw-ing'. The use of verbs helps the transition from scene-setting to action. For example, 'lined up' and 'stood' are slow, stative verbs, but 'whirled up' and 'circled' are energetic, active verbs that snap the reader out of the silent, rather static scene.

K E Y TERM **Narrative craft** – the techniques and devices used by a writer to create different effects as they relate events, describe characters and scenes

The next extract is the opening to a novel. This part of the story is told by a character, Mr Lockwood. (Another character, Nelly Dean, later shares the narrative role.)

1801—I have just returned from a visit to my landlord—the solitary neighbour that I shall be troubled with. This is certainly a beautiful country! In all England I do not believe that I could have fixed on a situation so completely removed from the stir of society. A perfect *misanthropist's Heaven—and Mr. Heathcliff and I are such a suitable pair to divide the desolation between us. A capital fellow! He little imagined how my heart warmed towards him when I beheld his black eyes withdraw so suspiciously under their brows, as I rode up, and when his fingers sheltered themselves, with a jealous resolution, still further in his waistcoat, as I announced my name.

 'Mr Heathcliff?' I said.

 A nod was the answer.

* misanthropist – someone who dislikes and avoids human company

From *Wuthering Heights* by Emily Brontë

In this extract, we see everything through the eyes of the narrator, Mr Lockwood. As the novel progresses, we realize that Mr Lockwood is well educated and intelligent, and so his narration of events, however bizarre, is given credibility.

K E Y TERM **Narrative voice** – the voice that tells the story and gives an account of events. A first-person narrator gives his or her first-hand account of events. A third-person narrator stands outside the story and tends to be more objective and often is omniscient (all seeing) and able to show the reader the thoughts of all the characters. More than one narrative voice can be used in the same text.

CORE TEXT

The next passage is the opening to a story, which is set in California, USA, in the 1930s.

A few miles south of Soledad, the Salinas river drops in close to the hillside bank and runs deep and green. The water is warm too, for it has slipped twinkling over the yellow sands in the sunlight before reaching the narrow pool. On one side of the river the golden foothill slopes curve up to the strong and rocky Gabilan mountains, but on the valley side the water is lined with trees—willows fresh and green with every spring, carrying in their lower leaf junctures the debris of the winter's flooding; and sycamores with mottled, white, recumbent limbs and branches that arch over the pool. On the sandy bank under the trees the leaves lie deep and so crisp that a lizard makes a great skittering if he runs among them. Rabbits come out of the brush to sit on the sand in the evening, and the damp flats are covered with the night tracks of 'coons, and with the spread pads of dogs from the ranches, and with the split-wedge tracks of deer that come to drink in the dark.

There is a path through the willows and among the sycamores, a path beaten hard by boys coming down from the ranches to swim in the deep pool, and beaten hard by tramps who come wearily down from the highway in the evening to *jungle-up near water. In front of the low horizontal limb of a giant sycamore there is an ashpile made by many fires; the limb is worn smooth by men who have sat on it.

Evening of a hot day started the little wind to moving among the leaves. The shade climbed up the hills toward the top. On the sandbanks the rabbits sat as quietly as little grey, sculptured stones. And then from the direction of the state highway came the sound of footsteps on crisp sycamore leaves. The rabbits hurried noiselessly for cover. A stilted heron laboured up into the air and pounded down river. For a moment the place was lifeless, and then two men emerged from the path and came into the opening by the green pool.

They had walked in single file down the path, and even in the open one stayed behind the other. Both men were dressed in denim trousers and in denim coats with brass buttons. Both wore black, shapeless hats and both carried tight blanket rolls slung over their shoulders. The first man was small and quick, dark of face, with restless eyes and sharp, strong features. Every part of him was defined: small, strong hands, slender arms, a thin and bony nose. Behind him walked his opposite, a huge man, shapeless of face, with large, pale eyes, with wide, sloping shoulders; and he walked heavily, dragging his feet a little, the way a bear drags his paws. His arms did not swing at his sides, but hung loosely.

The first man stopped short in the clearing, and the follower nearly ran over him. He took off his hat and wiped the sweat-band with his forefinger and snapped the moisture off. His huge companion dropped his blankets and flung himself down and drank from the surface of the green pool; drank with long gulps, snorting into the water like a horse. The small man stepped nervously beside him.

'Lennie!' he said sharply. 'Lennie, for God's sakes don't drink so much.' Lennie continued to snort into the pool. The small man leaned over and shook him by the shoulder. 'Lennie. You gonna be sick like you was last night.'

Lennie dipped his whole head under, hat and all, and then he sat up on the bank and his hat dripped down on his blue coat and ran down his back. 'Tha's good,' he said. 'You drink some, George. You take a good big drink.' He smiled happily.

George unslung his bindle and dropped it gently on the bank. 'I ain't sure it's good water,' he said. 'Looks kinda scummy.'

Lennie dabbled his big paw in the water and wiggled his fingers so the water arose in little splashes; rings widened across the pool to the other side and came back again.

---

* jungle-up – make a camp for the night

From *Of Mice and Men* by John Steinbeck

Getting started

ACTIVITIES

1 List the references to light and colour in the first three sentences. What impression do they create of the setting?

2 Look closely at this extract from the dialogue:

'Lennie. You gonna be sick like you was last night.'

Rewrite this in Standard English. Why do you think Steinbeck uses colloquial (non-standard) forms of English in speech?

Development

ACTIVITIES

3 Steinbeck uses powerful verbs to create the scene. For example:

'A stilted heron laboured up into the air and pounded down river.'

How do the verbs help the reader develop a picture of the scene? Find other examples, in the passage, where the writer's verbs enhance the scene.

4 Steinbeck uses several figurative devices to help the reader develop an image of the scene and keep them interested. Find examples of simile, metaphor, personification and onomatopoeia, and comment on the effectiveness of each device.

Extension

ACTIVITIES

5 Paragraphs 1 and 2 are written in the present tense but the start of paragraph 3 moves to the past tense. What effect does this have on your reading?

6 Consider the narrative voice in the passage. Who is telling the story? What advantages are there in using this type of narrative voice?

7 Steinbeck uses animal imagery in several places to refer to Lennie. Find three examples and comment on how effective you find them in revealing Lennie's character.

Additional study

ACTIVITY

Steinbeck usually opens each chapter in *Of Mice and Men* by setting the scene through his narration, and then allowing the action to unfold through his characters and their speech. If you have access to a copy of the novel, look at how he does this. This narrative technique is often employed by dramatists. Find an example from a piece of drama and compare the writer's techniques with those used by Steinbeck.

COMPARISON TEXT

Here is an account of a few years in the life of Quoyle, born in Brooklyn and raised in a shuffle of dreary upstate towns.

Hive-spangled, gut roaring with gas and cramp, he survived childhood; at the state university, hand clapped over his chin, he camouflaged torment with smiles and silence. Stumbled through his twenties and into his thirties learning to separate his feelings from his life, counting on nothing. He ate prodigiously, liked a ham knuckle, buttered spuds.

His jobs: distributor of vending machine candy, all-night clerk in a convenience store, a third-rate newspaperman. At thirty-six, bereft, brimming with grief and thwarted love, Quoyle steered away to Newfoundland, the rock that had generated his ancestors, a place he had never been nor thought to go.

A watery place. And Quoyle feared water, could not swim. Again and again the father had broken his clenched grip and thrown him into pools, brooks, lakes and surf. Quoyle knew the flavour of brack and waterweed.

From this youngest son's failure to dog-paddle the father saw other failures multiply like an explosion of virulent cells—failure to speak clearly; failure to sit up straight; failure to get up in the morning; failure in attitude; failure in ambition and ability; indeed, in everything. His own failure.

From *The Shipping News* by Annie Proulx

ACTIVITY   Compare Steinbeck and Proulx's narrative styles considering effects achieved. Think about:

◆ which extract is more descriptive and visual in style
◆ which extract is the less conventional in structure
◆ sentence structures
◆ pace and tone
◆ the narrative voices.

FURTHER READING

Emily Brontë, *Wuthering Heights* (Oxford World's Classics, OUP, 1998)
Daniel Defoe, *Moll Flanders* (Oxford World's Classics, OUP, 1998)
William Golding, *Lord of the Flies* (Faber and Faber, 1997)
Laurie Lee, *Cider with Rosie* (Penguin, 1998)
Annie Proulx, *The Shipping News* (Fourth Estate, 2002)
J.D. Salinger, *The Catcher in the Rye* (Penguin, 1994)

1: USING STANDARD AND NON-STANDARD FORMS FOR EFFECT

INTRODUCTION

English is the official language in more than 60 countries. English spoken in one country is often slightly different from English spoken in another country. In fact, within each country, there are differences in how English is spoken. Think of some television programmes that come from, or are set in, different regions within the United Kingdom – the accents and dialects vary.

KEY TERM

Standard English – a variety of English, not associated with any particular region, but with commonly accepted grammar, vocabulary, spelling and punctuation, and which is generally taught in schools. Standard English is used in courts, in books, broadsheet newspapers, and on formal television and radio programmes, for example the News. Standard English is generally the most widely understood and printed form of English. It is often associated with authority and an educated social class. Note that Standard English can be spoken with any accent.

KEY TERM

Non-standard English – varieties of English that are different from Standard English in dialect (grammar and vocabulary that are associated with a specific region), or pitch of formality, e.g. slang or colloquial lanaguage. In dictionaries, words that are non-standard English are often described as 'informal'.

The following extract is from *Wuthering Heights* by Emily Brontë. Cathy has declared her love for Edgar Linton in Heathcliff's hearing. Heathcliff, who loves Cathy, has disappeared. The servants, Joseph and Nelly Dean (the narrator), are asked to go and search for Heathcliff.

> I departed to renew my search; its result was disappointment, and Joseph's quest ended in the same.
>
> 'Yon lad gets war und war!' observed he on re-entering. 'He's left th' gate at t' full swing, and Miss's pony has trodden dahn two rigs o' corn, and plottered through, raight o'er into t' meadow! Hahsomdiver, t' maister 'ull play t' devil to-morn, and he'll do weel. He's patience itsseln wi' sich careless, offald craters – patience itsseln he is! Bud he'll not be soa allus – yah's see, all on ye! Yah mun'n't drive him out of his heead for nowt!'

> 'Have you found Heathcliff, you ass?' interrupted Catherine. 'Have you been looking for him, as I ordered?'
>
> 'I sud more likker look for th' horse,' he replied. 'It 'ud be to more sense. Bud I can look for norther horse nur man of a neeght loike this – as black as t' chimbley! und Heathcliff's noan t' chap to coom at MY whistle – happen he'll be less hard o' hearing wi' YE!'

ACTIVITY Working individually, or in a small group, complete the following tasks.

◆ Explain how Brontë allows the reader to 'hear' Joseph's accent.

◆ Compare Cathy's speech with Joseph's. What social distinctions might Brontë be making?

◆ Rework Joseph's dialectal speech into Standard English. List the changes that you make to word order, spellings, and vocabulary.

◆ What is gained and what is lost if the new version is used in the context of Brontë's story?

CORE TEXT

Read the poem *from* 'Unrelated Incidents' by Tom Leonard (it is in the AQA *Anthology*, Specification A). The poem is written in non-standard form for effect. Think about the effect that the poet is aiming to create. Consider the tone and purpose of the poem.

Getting started

ACTIVITIES 1 Tom Leonard uses his Scottish dialect in the poem. Find three examples where you think this is apparent. Why do you think he wants this dialect to be heard?

2 The poet uses the slang word 'scruff' on three occasions. Explain why you think he uses a non-standard word and why it is repeated three times.

Development

ACTIVITIES 3 Many of the words in the poem are of one or two syllables. Select three lines that contain short words and explore what effects these have on the pace and tone of the poem.

4 Leonard uses many short words with strong vowel sounds in them. Find a few examples of this and explain what effect this has on the tone of the poem.

5 In written Standard English we expect to see capital letters and punctuation. Tom Leonard uses no capital letters and very little punctuation. What effects do you think he wants to create?

Extension

ACTIVITIES **6** Think about the layout and structure of the poem. Clarify your thoughts by copying and completing the grid below.

Technique	Example	Effect
Enjambement		
Length of sentences		
Final sentence		
Other points		

7 Tom Leonard's poem is written in a Scottish dialect yet the reader can still understand it. Why do you think he chose to use a non-standard form to relay his message?

ADDITIONAL STUDY

ACTIVITY Rewrite the poem in Standard English. Remember you can:

- ◆ change words and phrases
- ◆ add punctuation
- ◆ alter sentence lengths
- ◆ change the layout of the poem.

Compare your new version with the original and examine:

- ◆ whether the message is still clear to the reader
- ◆ if the tone of the poem has changed
- ◆ whether a different layout alters the impact of the poem.

COMPARISON TEXTS

Text 1

When Jesus heard what had happened, he withdrew by boat privately to a solitary place. Hearing of this, the crowds followed him on foot from the towns. When Jesus landed and saw a large crowd, he had compassion on them and healed their sick.

As evening approached, the disciples came to him and said, 'This is a remote place, and it's already getting late. Send the crowds away, so that they can go to the villages and buy themselves some food.'

Jesus replied, 'They do not need to go away. You give them something to eat.'

'We have here only five loaves of bread and two fish,' they answered.

From the Bible (The New International Version) Matthew 14: 13-21

Text 2

Jesus' chinas met up with 'im, and they told him all they'd done, and all about their preaching. There were so many people about that Jesus and his little group of apostles didn't even have time for a bite to eat. So 'e said to 'em, 'Oi fellas, let's pop off on our Jack for a while and have a little rest and a kip.' So they got into a nanny and headed off to a quiet place.

   Loads of people saw them leaving – people from all the different towns, who ran like the clappers by land, and arrived at the same place Jesus was headed for. But they arrived before Jesus and his mates did. So when Jesus got out of the old nanny, 'e saw this bloomin' huge crowd , and he felt sorry for them, 'cos they were like little lost sheep without a shepherd. Jesus started to teach them loads of things. Now time was getting on, and a little alligator his disciples came up to him and said, 'It's getting a little bit late, boss, and this is a really lonely place. We think we should send all these people to some of the farms and villages dahn the old frog so that they can buy some nosh to eat.'

   'Why don't you give 'em something to eat?' Jesus asked.

   'Now hang on, boss,' they said. 'Are we gonna have to spend two hundred silver coins on Uncle Fred in order to feed this lot?'

   Jesus asked, 'How much grub 'ave you got? Go an' 'ave a butcher's.' After they'd 'ad a look, they came back and told 'im, 'We've got five loaves of Uncle Fred and two Lilian Gish.'

From *The Bible in Cockney* by Mike Coles

Text 3

Wen jesus herd wat had hapend, he wthdru by boat privtly 2 a solitry plce. Hearing of ths, v crowds folowd him on ft frm v twns. Wen jesus lnded and saw a lrge crowd, he felt sorry 4 thm and healed thr sick.

   As evning aprochd, v dsipls cam to hm & sed, "ths is a rmot plce, & its alrdy getng l8. Snd v crowds away, so tht they cn go 2 v villages & buy thmslvs som food." Jesus rplied "they do nt need 2 go away. U gve thm somthng to eat."

   "We hav here only 5 loaves of bread & 2 fish." Thy ansd.

ACTIVITY Think about the different audiences for these texts. For whom do you think they were written? What do you think were the authors' purposes in writing these texts in these different formats?

Compare and contrast all three texts, focusing on:

◆ structures (sentences) and length
◆ language variation
◆ register – formality and informality
◆ standard and non-standard forms.

Further reading

The Bible in Cockney by Mike Coles (The Bible Reading Fellowship, 2001)

Hobson's Choice by Harold Brighouse (Heinemann, 1992)

Wuthering Heights by Emily Brontë (Oxford World's Classics OUP, 1998)

R father n hvn (up 2 d8 txts frm d bible) edited by Simon Jenkins (Westminster John Knox Press, Louisville and London, 2002)

Basic Broad Yorkshire by Arnold Kellett (Smith Settle, 1991)

Ee By Gum Lord! By Arnold Kellett (Smith Settle, 1996)

Educating Rita by Willy Russell (Methuen, 2001)

Pygmalion by George Bernard Shaw (Penguin, 2000)

2: EXPLORING DIFFERENT STYLES OF WRITING

INTRODUCTION

Think of the range of writing that we come across in a typical day: recipes on packets of food; instructions how to make things work; recounts of events in newspapers and magazines; gossip and practical information sent in emails or text messages; diary entries; formal letters. Think of other examples and list them.

You will have already explored a range of writing while completing coursework and preparing for the examination:

Component	Strand	Range of writing
Coursework	Original Writing	Explore, imagine, entertain
	Media	Analyse, review, comment
Examination	English Paper 1	Argue, persuade, advise
	English Paper 2	Inform, explain, describe

This section looks in detail at different styles of writing within the range. It will focus in particular on six different styles (formal, informal, personal, impersonal, technical, and non-technical), although there are, of course, others.

CORE TEXTS

ACTIVITY The following extracts are written in different styles (listed in the grid below). As you read them, identify which text is written in which style. Copy and complete the list below, listing the features that helped you to make your choice.

Text style	Text Number	Features
Formal text		
Informal text		
Personal text		
Impersonal text		
Technical text		
Non-technical text		

1

By the 1980s Judi had scaled the highest pinnacles in the theatre – she was the leading lady at the National and had won a clutch of the most prestigious stage awards. But her handful of appearances in the cinema was limited to often quite small supporting roles, in art-house movies that were never contenders for huge box office success. She had virtually written off any thought of a significant film career, when she was suddenly offered the part of the spy chief 'M' in the first Bond movie to star Pierce Brosnan as 007 – *Goldeneye*.

From *Judi Dench* by Jonathan Miller

2

Lunchtime quake shakes Manchester

Greater Manchester has been hit by a series of 13 earthquakes and aftershocks, the latest measuring 2.5 on the Richter scale.

The most recent tremor hit the city at about 1326 BST on Tuesday.

It lasted around three seconds and caused buildings to shake.

Julian Bukits, a seismologist from the British Geological Survey (BGS), told BBC News Online: "We are analysing the data to find out the magnitude, but from what witnesses are saying it was a significant event – perhaps as strong as the first one on Monday."

It follows the four tremors which hit the city on Monday, one of which measured 3.9 on the Richter scale.

From BBC News Online 22-10-02

3

WHIRLWIND VORTEX (also known as PLASMA VORTEX)

The first theory proposed by Dr Terrence Meaden in the 1980s attempted to explain all spirally generated circle patterns as a product of entirely natural atmospheric phenomena. Meaden likened the vortex to dustdevils, tornados, etc., but also including friction-generated plasma which could account for the anomalous light phenomena which many eyewitnesses had seen. Meaden claimed the forces involved were hitherto "unrecognized helical or toroidal forces" which had "subsidiary electromagnetic properties due to self-electrification." The vortex would presumably form high above the ground, then suddenly "breakdown" to the ground level in an axial strike. The theory was plausible for a number of years, with further corroboration obtained in Japan by Dr Y.H. Ohtsuki and Prof. H. Ofuruton. Their lab research produced similar vortices by electrostatic discharge and microwave interference. Theoretical work on the plasma-vortex was carried out by Prof. H. Kikuchi, Japan, who modelled the vortex using energy potentials including an interaction term between an axial electric field and the earth's magnetic field.

From http://www.paradigmshift.com/theories.html

4

Low-fat Moist Carrot Cake

Begin by whisking the 6 oz (175 g) sugar, eggs and oil together in a bowl using an electric hand whisk for 2–3 minutes. Then sift together the flour, bicarbonate of soda and the mixed spice into the bowl, tipping in all the bits of bran that are left in the sieve. Now stir all this together, then fold in the orange zest, carrots and sultanas. After that, pour the mixture into the prepared tin and bake on the centre shelf of the oven for 35–40 minutes, until it is well risen and feels firm and springy to the touch when lightly pressed in the centre.

While the cake is cooking, make the topping by mixing all the ingredients in a bowl until light and fluffy, then cover with clingfilm and chill for 1–2 hours or until needed.

Now you need to make the syrup glaze, and to do this whisk together the fruit juices and sugar in a bowl. Then, when the cake comes out of the oven, stab it all over with a skewer and quickly spoon the syrup over as evenly as possible. Now leave the cake on one side to cool in the tin, during which time the syrup will be absorbed. Then, when the cake is completely cold, remove it from the tin, spread the topping over, cut it into 12 squares and dust with a little more cinnamon.

From *How to Cook*, Book One by Delia Smith BBC Books

5

We're all shook oop

By LYNDSEY WEATHERALL and JILL MOWAT

FOUR earthquakes rocked MANCHESTER yesterday — and rumbled on the cobbles of Coronation Street.

Experts were shocked by the tremors that damaged houses and hit the 'oop north' TV soap during filming at city centre studios.

Chimneys throughout the area tumbled and goods were hurled off shop shelves when the first quake struck at 8.45am — the height of the morning rush-hour.

Workers were evacuated as fire alarms were set off by the quake measuring 3.2 on the Richter scale.

A slightly smaller one followed 19 minutes later measuring 2.3.

But nearly four hours later, at 12.42, the city was rocked AGAIN by a tremor even larger than the first.

This hit 3.9 on the Richter scale and was immediately followed by another hitting 3.5.

There were no reports of serious injuries in the quakes. The epicentre of the first two was Beswick, one mile east of the city centre and home of the sports stadium built for this year's Commonwealth Games.

From *The Sun* 22-10-02

6

Stephen Evans, the BBC's North America Business Correspondent was in the World Trade Centre in New York when the first plane struck on September 11 2001. He was meant to be interviewing someone but his plans soon changed…

I was a little early so I was sitting languidly in the vast lobby, passing the time reading the *New York Times*, when there was a loud thud, something like a huge iron door slamming shut or a large container full of concrete crashing from high above. The walls shuddered. I had to tell myself: 'Those walls really did shake. I felt it.' I thought: 'Earthquake? No, that's San Francisco. This is New York.'

A film of smoke descended on the piazza. People streamed past me through the lobby. I turned my mini-disc recorder on to capture the sound of what was happening, scrabbling with the machine's tangle of cables on the marble floor before joining the exodus. Strangely, no one was screaming at this point, no one was panicking – there was just a determined movement away from trouble.

From *The Day that Shook the World* BBC Books

Getting started

ACTIVITIES 1 Copy the chart below, then focus on the formal and informal reports based on the Manchester earthquake. Complete the chart, bearing in mind that some boxes may be left blank as the technique could be relevant to just one text.

Technique	Example and effect		Example and effect	
	Formal	effect	Informal	effect
Headline				
Use of verbs				
Build up of drama				
Emotive language				
Informal tone and style				
Formal tone and style				
Repetitive feel				
Capitalization of words				
Quotations				

2 Using the chart for reference, explain the differences between formal and informal reportage.

3 Which of these two texts do you think gives the reader the greater insight into the events? Explain your views.

Development

ACTIVITIES 4 Copy the chart below, then focus on the personal and impersonal passages. Complete the chart, bearing in mind that some boxes may be left blank as the technique could be relevant to just one text.

Technique	Example and effect		Example and effect	
	Formal	effect	Informal	effect
Tense used				
Narrative voice				
Use of imagery				
Detail and description				
Powerful language				
Verbs to suit scene				
Sense of person involved				

5 How would you explain to someone the differences between personal and impersonal writing? Write a short explanation.

6 What do you think makes the personal text so powerful?

Extension

ACTIVITIES 7 Copy the chart below, then focus on the technical and non-technical extracts. Complete the chart, bearing in mind that some boxes may be left blank as the technique could be relevant to just one text.

Technique	Example and effect		Example and effect	
	Technical	effect	Non-technical	effect
Use of temporal connectives to sequence text				
Use of imperative form of verb				
Comparison to make point clear				
Detailed noun phrases				
Quotations				
Vocabulary to suit subject				
References to subject specialists				
Compound sentences				
Long, complex sentences				

8 Looking at all six extracts, which one do you think:

  ◆ is the most entertaining to read?
  ◆ gives the strongest sense of how the writer felt?
  ◆ is the simplest to follow?
  ◆ is most direct and to the point?
  ◆ is the most detailed and complex?

Give examples and explanations to support your answers.

9 A style of writing is usually selected to suit a specific audience. Who would you say is the target audience for each of the six texts? Explain the reasoning behind your answers, referring to the texts themselves.

ADDITIONAL STUDY

ACTIVITY Rework the personal passage (6, by Steven Evans) into an impersonal style. What do you lose in your new version? Write a short analysis of the effect of the changes you have made.

COMPARISON

ACTIVITY Select at least two styles of writing and find an example of each. These might be from books, magazines, websites, or newspapers. Once you have selected them, compare and contrast them in terms of:

- structural devices (layout, sentence types and lengths)
- linguistic devices (figurative, technical, descriptive, etc.)
- stylistic conventions (formal, informal, personal, impersonal, etc.)
- any other interesting points (to reach the top grade).

This is good preparation for English Paper 1 Section A where you will be expected to study and compare at least two texts.

FURTHER READING

Broadsheet newspapers (formal texts) such as *The Guardian*; *The Independent*; *The Times,* etc.

Tabloid newspapers (informal texts) such as *The Sun*; *The Mirror*, *The News of the World*.

Personal texts such as *Anne Frank: The Diary of a Young Girl* (Penguin, 2000); *The Faber Book of Diaries* (Faber, 1989); autobiographies

Impersonal texts such as biographies; reports; and discursive writing

Technical texts such as specialist subjects; manuals for gadgets, etc.

Non-technical texts such as recipes; instructions on how to operate a household item

1: Structural and presentational devices

Introduction

Texts are presented in specific ways to suit particular audiences and to achieve certain effects. As readers, we make judgements about texts just by glancing at their layout, key words and images, before we even read the texts themselves. We often decide what sort of text type it is, purely on layout. Look at the three templates below. Without any text, colour or images, you can probably still identify which is an advert which is a web page and which is a newspaper report.

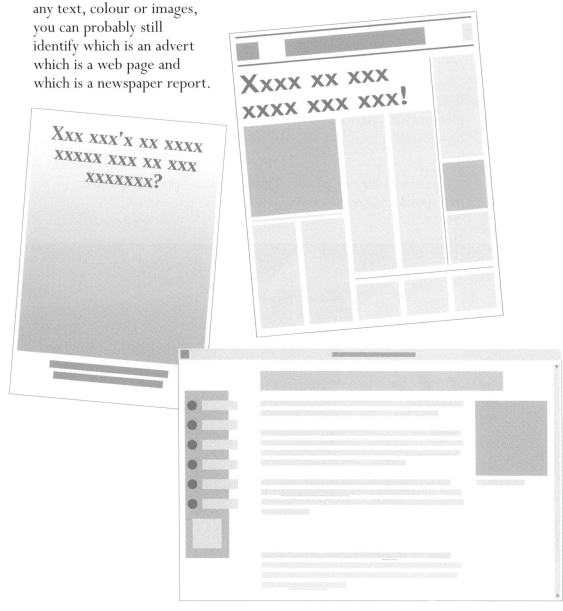

Layout is a basic form of presentational device. Other visual devices that writers and designers employ to give texts impact are:

- colour
- borders, panels, boxes
- different fonts and font sizes
- artwork and photographs
- logos
- headings and subheadings.

In texts which compete for a reader's attention, for example advertisements, writers need to present their text in a succinct, very accessible way. They also want to make their text memorable, and evoke a positive response from the reader, so they often use wit and humour. Presentational devices are highly crafted in most adverts, and the effects of the presentation are often subtle, making use of the reader's associations and targeting an audience of a specific gender and age.

In this section, we look at three adverts, analyzing the impact of their presentational devices, both visual and textual. Similar analysis could be undertaken with any effective adverts.

CORE TEXTS

Look at the following adverts. Think about the presentational devices they use to convey their message to specific audiences.

1

2

ANNE BOLEYN, PERFECTLY EXECUTED. BY ROYAL MAIL.

Henry VIII was handsome, a famous musician and King of England. Some women really lost their heads over him.

If only they'd known about Special Stamps, they're a much better catch.

Anne was Henry's second wife and their union transformed British history. To marry her, he divorced Catherine of Aragon, angering the Pope. The King wrenched power away from Rome and created the Church of England.

Such momentous events deserve momentous issues. So, a huge amount of skill, time and effort is invested in every single Special Stamp we produce.

After all, The Great Tudor range isn't the only one to feature masterpieces. We often work with the world's best contemporary artists.

From an initial design, hundreds of sketches are produced. Some, like Anne, are given the chop.

Only one set is chosen.

Even then, our work isn't finished. The stamps have to be printed by one of the few specialist companies who can achieve the high standards we require. Next, each printed stamp has to pass a number of quality checks to ensure that each is perfect.

Finally, they have to be approved by the Queen herself.

You can collect Mint Stamps, or informative, decorative First Day Covers and Presentation Packs.

Join The British Philatelic Bureau. You'll find it's great for anyone who'd like to know more about Special Stamps.

So, be decisive, like Henry VIII, take a sharp object and . . .

Off with the coupon.

PLEASE SEND ME MORE INFORMATION ABOUT THE BRITISH PHILATELIC BUREAU.

Mr/Mrs/Miss/Ms/Other _____ First name _____ Surname _____

Address _____

_____

Postcode _____ Telephone _____

Please return to British Philatelic Bureau, Freepost, Edinburgh EH3 OHN.

Royal Mail

3

Come face to face with hand to hand.

IN REAL LIFE (and death) the battlefield was a far from romantic arena, as you'll discover when you visit 'Death or Glory' at Warwick Castle. You'll get the chance to try on a helmet, feel the weight of a sword and discover the sheer amount of strength needed to flex the deadly longbow.

At the same time you'll feel your senses stirred as the clamour of battles, from the Mediaeval Wars to the Napoleonic Campaigns, rises around you, and you learn for yourself the reality of how soldiers lived and died on the field.

This attraction houses more than 1000 pieces of arms and armour collected at the Castle over hundreds of years.

> TWO MILES FROM JUNCTION 15 OF THE M40
>
> FOR DETAILS CALL 01926 406609
>
> www.warwick-castle.co.uk
>
> OPEN EVERY DAY EXCEPT CHRISTMAS DAY

WARWICK CASTLE
The secret life of England

Then for a behind the scenes look at the strategy and preparation involved in warfare, move to our Kingmaker attraction and see a 15th century army preparing for The Battle of Barnet. And if you're still feeling brave and bold after that, dare yourself to enter the eerie 14th century Ghost Tower.

Alternatively, you could leave the blood and thunder behind and mingle with the rich and famous of Victorian society in 'A Royal Weekend Party, 1898'.

Warwick Castle is crammed to the turrets with 1000 years of real history, so why not mobilise your troops and start planning your attack now?

Getting started

ACTIVITIES

1 Copy and complete the grid below, adding your own list of presentational devices in the first column. Remember to consider both visual layout and textual features.

Presentational devices	Advert 1	Advert 2	Advert 3

2 Select five devices from the last activity and comment on the effectiveness of each one, considering why it has been used. Remember, effective devices help to ensure that a strong message reaches the intended audience.

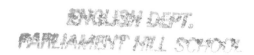

Development

ACTIVITIES

3 Visual images are sometimes more effective in catching the reader's initial attention than words. Which advert has the most striking image in your opinion? Which one has the most striking language?

4 The advert that you find most effective may not have the same impact on another reader. Look carefully at the language used in each advert and at the pictures. Describe the audience (age, gender, circumstances) that you think might find each advert most effective.

Extension

ACTIVITIES

5 Look at the headings in adverts 2 and 3. How is language used? What effects do you think the writer wanted to create?

6 Cartoons are usually light-hearted forms of entertainment. Why do you think the NSPCC chose to use a cartoon child in their advert when the message is so serious?

7 The presentation of the adverts is closely linked to their target audience. How you would change the presentation (visual and textual) of the Warwick Castle advert if you wanted to target it at an elderly audience, or change the stamp advert if you wanted to target it at children?

ADDITIONAL STUDY

ACTIVITY

Compare the ways meaning is conveyed in text, image and layout in all three adverts. Which one do you find most effective and why?

COMPARISON TEXT

ACTIVITY

Choose one of the following activities.

1 Using at least three DVD or video box covers, analyze and comment on the uses of language, image and layout to convey meaning. How do these differ from the adverts in this section?

2 Select three adverts (either on television or printed) that are targeted at specific audiences. Review and analyze how each one is tailored to its specific audience.

3 Select one type of advert from the list below and find a range of adverts within that type.
  ◆ film adverts   ◆ adverts for teenagers   ◆ adverts about football

Which advert do you think is the most successful? Explain your choice.

2: Effects of dramatic devices and structures

Introduction

Dramatists use a range of dramatic devices and structures to create effects. These include:

◆ revealing a character's inner thoughts and feelings through soliloquy
◆ using a narrator or chorus to give a prologue or commentary on the developing drama
◆ juxtaposing (placing side by side) contrasting scenes
◆ giving hints of things to come in the plot (foreshadowing)
◆ using short staccato sentences to increase tension, or long complex ones to build detail or decrease tension
◆ allowing the audience to see and know more than a character (dramatic irony).

Look at these short extracts from Shakespeare plays.

> **1** This castle hath a pleasant seat

From *Macbeth* Act 1 Scene 6 (Spoken by the king, Duncan)

Here, Shakespeare uses dramatic irony. When King Duncan arrives at Macbeth's castle and says that the place is well located (and he likes it) the audience already knows that Macbeth is plotting to murder Duncan and that the castle will be far from 'pleasant'.

KEY TERM

Dramatic irony – a form of irony in drama in which the audience knows more about a character's situation than the character does.

> **2** How if, when I am laid into the tomb,
> I wake before the time that Romeo
> Come to redeem me? There's a fearful point!
> Shall I not then be stifl'd in the vault,
> To whose foul mouth no healthsome air breathes in,
> And there die strangl'd ere my Romeo comes?

From *Romeo and Juliet* Act 4 Scene 3 (Spoken by Juliet)

This soliloquy develops a close relationship between the character and audience. Juliet reveals her secret fears and anxieties, and as an audience, our sympathy is stirred.

KEY TERM

Soliloquy – where a character speaks his or her thoughts aloud, alone on the stage

CORE TEXT

Read through the extract below. It contains Act 2 Scenes 2 and 3 from *Macbeth* by William Shakespeare. Macbeth has just murdered the king, Duncan. Lady Macbeth (Macbeth's wife) is awaiting his arrival after committing the murder at the start of the first scene.

The questions at the end of the extract will help you analyze the effects of the dramatic structures and devices, but you may wish to prepare for these by highlighting specific features as you read. (You could photocopy the extract and annotate it for easy reference.) Highlight any features that you feel enhance the drama. These might include:

- soliloquies
- contrast of characters and moods
- different types of language spoken by different characters
- humour and suspense
- varying sentence lengths and types for effect
- dramatic irony.

Scene 2
Macbeth's *castle; enter* Lady Macbeth

LADY MACBETH
  That which hath made them drunk, hath made me bold;
  What hath quench'd them, hath given me fire.

  An owl shrieks

                                          Hark, peace!
  It was the owl that shriek'd, the fatal bellman
  Which gives the stern'st good-night. He is about it.
  The doors are open, and the surfeited grooms   5
  Do mock their charge with snores. I have drugg'd their possets,
  That death and nature do contend about them,
  Whether they live, or die.

  Enter Macbeth *with two bloody daggers*

MACBETH   Who's there? What ho?

LADY MACBETH   Alack, I am afraid they have awak'd,
  And 'tis not done; th'attempt and not the deed   10
  Confounds us. Hark! I laid their daggers ready,
  He could not miss 'em. Had he not resembled
  My father as he slept, I had done't. My husband?

MACBETH   I have done the deed. Didst thou not hear a noise?

LADY MACBETH   I heard the owl scream and the crickets cry. 15
  Did not you speak?

MACBETH   When?

LADY MACBETH   Now.

MACBETH   As I descended?

LADY MACBETH   Ay.   20

MACBETH   Hark, who lies i'th'second chamber?

LADY MACBETH   Donaldbain.

MACBETH   This is a sorry sight.

LADY MACBETH   A foolish thought, to say a sorry sight.

MACBETH
  There's one did laugh in's sleep, and one cried 'Murder!', 25
  That they did wake each other; I stood, and heard them,
  But they did say their prayers and address'd them
  Again to sleep.

LADY MACBETH   There are two lodg'd together.

MACBETH   One cried 'God bless us!' and 'Amen' the other,
  As they had seen me with these hangman's hands.   30
  List'ning their fear, I could not say 'Amen'
  When they did say 'God bless us.'

LADY MACBETH   Consider it not so deeply.

MACBETH   But wherefore could not I pronounce 'Amen'?
I had most need of blessing and 'Amen'   35
Stuck in my throat.

LADY MACBETH   These deeds must not be thought
After these ways; so, it will make us mad.

MACBETH   Methought I heard a voice cry, 'Sleep no more:
Macbeth does murder sleep', the innocent sleep,
Sleep that knits up the ravell'd sleeve of care,   40
The death of each day's life, sore labour's bath,
Balm of hurt minds, great nature's second course,
Chief nourisher in life's feast.

LADY MACBETH   What do you mean?

MACBETH   Still it cried, 'Sleep no more' to all the house;
'Glamis hath murder'd sleep', and therefore Cawdor   45
Shall sleep no more: Macbeth shall sleep no more.

LADY MACBETH
Who was it, that thus cried? Why, worthy thane,
You do unbend your noble strength to think
So brain-sickly of things. Go get some water
And wash this filthy witness from your hand.   50
Why did you bring these daggers from the place?
They must lie there. Go carry them and smear
The sleepy grooms with blood.

MACBETH   I'll go no more.
I am afraid to think what I have done;
Look on't again, I dare not.   55

LADY MACBETH   Infirm of purpose!
Give me the daggers. The sleeping and the dead
Are but as pictures; 'tis the eye of childhood
That fears a painted devil. If he do bleed,
I'll gild the faces of the grooms withal,
For it must seem their guilt.   60
                                                     [Exit

    Knock within

MACBETH   Whence is that knocking?
How is't with me, when every noise appals me?
What hands are here? Ha: they pluck out mine eyes.
Will all great Neptune's ocean wash this blood
Clean from my hand? No: this my hand will rather
The multitudinous seas incarnadine,   65
Making the green one red.

    Enter Lady Macbeth

LADY MACBETH   My hands are of your colour, but I shame
To wear a heart so white.

    Knock within

                                         I hear a knocking
At the south entry. Retire we to our chamber;
A little water clears us of this deed.   70
How easy is it then! Your constancy
Hath left you unattended.

    Knock within

                                    Hark, more knocking.
Get on your night-gown, lest occasion call us
And show us to be watchers. Be not lost
So poorly in your thoughts.   75

MACBETH   To know my deed, 'twere best not know my self.

    Knock within

Wake Duncan with thy knocking: I would thou couldst.
                                                   [Exeunt

Scene 3
    Macbeth's castle: enter a Porter. Knocking within

PORTER   Here's a knocking indeed: if a man were porter of
hell-gate, he should have old turning the key.

    Knock

Knock, knock, knock. Who's there i'th'name of Beelzebub?
Here's a farmer that hanged himself on th'expectation of
plenty. Come in time—have napkins enough about you,
here you'll sweat for't.

    Knock

Knock, knock. Who's there in th'other devil's name? Faith,
here's an equivocator that could swear in both the scales
against either scale, who committed treason enough for
God's sake, yet could not equivocate to heaven.   10
O, come in, equivocator.

    Knock

Knock, knock, knock. Who's there? Faith, here's an English
tailor come hither for stealing out of a French hose. Come
in, tailor, here you may roast your goose.

    Knock

Knock, knock. Never at quiet: what are you? But this place
is too cold for hell. I'll devil-porter it no further: I had
thought to have let in some of all professions that go the
primrose way to th'everlasting bonfire.

    Knock

Anon, anon. I pray you, remember the porter.

    Opens door

    Enter Macduff and Lennox

MACDUFF   Was it so late, friend, ere you went to bed,   20
That you do lie so late?

PORTER   Faith, sir, we were carousing till the second cock,
and drink, sir, is a great provoker of three things.

MACDUFF   What three things does drink especially provoke?

PORTER   Marry, sir, nose-painting, sleep, and urine. Lechery,
sir, it provokes, and unprovokes: it provokes the desire, but
it takes away the performance. Therefore much drink may
be said to be an equivocator with lechery: it makes him,
and it mars him: it sets him on, and it takes him off; it
persuades him and disheartens him, makes him   30
stand to and not stand to. In conclusion, equivocates
him in a sleep, and giving him the lie, leaves him.

MACDUFF   I believe drink gave thee the lie last night.

PORTER   That it did, sir, i'the very throat on me, but I
requited him for his lie, and, I think, being too strong for
him, though he took up my legs sometime, yet I made a
shift to cast him.

Enter Macbeth

MACDUFF   Is thy master stirring?
Our knocking has awak'd him: here he comes.
                                        [*Exit Porter*

LENNOX   Good morrow, noble sir.   40

MACBETH   Good morrow, both.

MACDUFF   Is the king stirring, worthy thane?

MACBETH   Not yet.

MACDUFF   He did command me to call timely on him;
I have almost slipp'd the hour.

MACBETH   I'll bring you to him.

MACDUFF
I know this is a joyful trouble to you, but yet 'tis one.

MACBETH
The labour we delight in physics pain. This is the door.

MACDUFF
I'll make so bold to call, for 'tis my limited service.
                                        [*Exit*

LENNOX   Goes the king hence today?

MACBETH   He does—he did appoint so.

LENNOX   The night has been unruly: where we lay,
Our chimneys were blown down, and, as they say,   50
Lamentings heard i'th'air, strange screams of death
And prophesying with accents terrible
Of dire combustion and confus'd events,

New hatch'd to th'woeful time. The obscure bird
Clamour'd the livelong night. Some say, the earth
Was feverous and did shake.

MACBETH   'Twas a rough night.

LENNOX   My young remembrance cannot parallel
A fellow to it.

Enter Macduff

MACDUFF   O horror, horror, horror,
Tongue nor heart cannot conceive, nor name thee.   60

MACBETH AND LENNOX   What's the matter?

MACDUFF   Confusion now hath made his masterpiece:
Most sacrilegious murder hath broke ope
The Lord's anointed temple and stole thence
The life o'th'building.

MACBETH   What is't you say, the life?

LENNOX   Mean you his majesty?

MACDUFF   Approach the chamber and destroy your sight
With a new Gorgon. Do not bid me speak:
See and then speak yourselves.   70
                        [*Exeunt* Macbeth *and* Lennox

                                Awake, awake!
Ring the alarum bell! Murder and treason!
Banquo and Donaldbain! Malcolm, awake,
Shake off his downy sleep, death's counterfeit,
And look on death itself. Up, up, and see
The great doom's image. Malcolm, Banquo,
As from your graves rise up and walk like sprites
To countenance this horror.

Bell rings. Enter Lady Macbeth

LADY MACBETH   What's the business
That such a hideous trumpet calls to parley
The sleepers of the house? Speak, speak.

MACDUFF   O gentle lady,
'Tis not for you to hear what I can speak.   80
The repetition in a woman's ear
Would murder as it fell.—

Enter Banquo

                                O Banquo, Banquo,
Our royal master's murder'd.

LADY MACBETH   Woe, alas,
What, in our house?

BANQUO   Too cruel, anywhere.
Dear Duff, I prithee contradict thyself
And say it is not so.

Try to identify other dramatic devices in addition to these.

Getting started

ACTIVITIES

1 Pick out examples from Lady Macbeth's opening soliloquy where she indicates the time of day. Why does Shakespeare do this?

2 Lady Macbeth's soliloquy is a dramatic device. Why do you think Shakespeare uses it at this point? What effect does it create? Think about how much information it conveys and the tension it creates.

3 Look at lines 16 to 25 in Scene 2. Shakespeare uses a range of short simple sentences and questions. What effect do these have? How might Shakespeare use this device to control the audience's reaction?

Development

ACTIVITIES

4 Re-read Macbeth's lines from 38 to 66 in Scene 2. Here, Shakespeare uses long complex sentences. What effect is created, especially after a run of short sentences? (Look back at lines 16 to 25.)

5 Re-read Scene 3 lines 68 to the end. Shakespeare uses dramatic irony twice. Locate these examples and explore why he uses this device.

6 Shakespeare often used poetry to express the words of characters with high social status, particularly when they were talking about exalted or important themes. He often used prose for characters further down the social scale, particularly if their ideas were bawdy, domestic or simple commentary. Explore how Shakespeare uses poetry and prose in these two scenes. What effects are created by switching between poetry and prose?

Extension

ACTIVITIES

7 Later in the play, Lady Macbeth becomes mentally unstable, imagining blood on her hands that will not come off. This event is foreshadowed in Scene 2. Can you spot where? What are the dramatic effects of this foreshadowing?

8 Scene 2 is about the murder of Duncan, whereas Scene 3 opens with a drunken porter. Shakespeare juxtaposes these scenes for dramatic effect. Examine the effects achieved.

9 Shakespeare controls the tension well in these two scenes. How does he achieve this? Focus on:
   ◆ pace (sentence structures)   ◆ use of language
   ◆ use of soliloquy   ◆ foreshadowing
   ◆ juxtaposition of scenes.

ADDITIONAL STUDY

There are several film versions of *Macbeth*:

◆ Orson Welles, 1939   ◆ Roman Polanski, 1971
◆ RSC (Judi Dench and Ian MCKellen), 1976.

ACTIVITY Watch Act 2 Scenes 2 and 3 in a film version. Explore which devices you feel the director best exploits for dramatic effect. Think about the devices covered in this unit:

◆ dramatic irony   ◆ soliloquy
◆ references to times of day   ◆ sentence types and lengths
◆ poetry and prose   ◆ foreshadowing
◆ juxtaposition of scene   ◆ use of language.

COMPARISON TEXT

Shakespeare uses a wealth of dramatic devices in all his plays but particularly in his opening scenes where he needs to capture his audience's attention promptly.

ACTIVITY Explore the range of devices by selecting two or three examples from the list below. Comment on the effectiveness of these devices and consider how successful you think they are in gaining the interest of an audience.

◆ *Hamlet* – Act 1 Scene 1
◆ *Macbeth* – Act 1 Scene 1
◆ *Henry V* – Prologue
◆ *Romeo and Juliet* – Prologue
◆ *The Tempest* – Act 1 Scene 1
◆ *The Merchant of Venice* – Act 1 Scene 1
◆ *The Winter's Tale* – Act 1 Scene 1

FURTHER READING

Christopher Marlowe, *Tamburlaine the Great*; *The Jew of Malta* (both in *Dr Faustus and Other Plays*, Oxford World's Classics, OUP, 1998)

Arthur Miller, *A View from the Bridge* and *All My Sons* (both Penguin Twentieth Century Classics, 2000); *The Crucible* (Penguin, 2000)

William Shakespeare, plays in the Oxford School Shakespeare series, OUP

George Bernard Shaw, *Pygmalion* (Penguin, 2000)

Tennessee Williams, *A Streetcar Named Desire* (Penguin, 2000); *The Glass Menagerie* (Methuen Drama, 2000)

3: Developing an argument

Introduction

In this unit you will examine the conventions and devices used by writers to develop an argument. You will explore how certain effects are achieved and look at prose and poetry texts in which argument is the central issue. The study of these examples should enhance your own analytical and writing skills.

Spelt out

Should we really care that our children cannot spell Shakespeare's name correctly? After all, neither could the great playwright himself. He used three different variants – Shakspere, Shakspeare, and Shakespeare. And as for not being able to spell, Jane Austen, the novelist, spelt 'stopped' as 'stopt', 'scissors' as 'scissars', and 'sofa' as 'sopha'. In fact, it wasn't until Austen's near contemporary, Samuel Johnson, published his *Dictionary* in 1775 that standardised spelling became a possibility, let alone a way of torturing school children, judging Scrabble entries and filling in crosswords. Yes, we too can see the practical advantages of removing ambiguities, but would that be sufficient reason to give-in to that modern instrument of standardisation – the Microsoft Spell Checker – with its insistence that 'defence' is spelt 'defense' and 'humour' as 'humor'? No, let a thousand variants bloom, in spelling as in all other forms of life.

From The *Independent*, September 4th 2002

The writer opens the argument with a direct rhetorical question. The effect is to gain the immediate attention of the reader as it challenges them to decide on their own viewpoint. The view that spelling does not matter is backed up with the evidence that even Shakespeare spelt his name in various ways. (Names, dates and statistics and are often used to give credibility to an argument.) This point is developed by referring to another great writer, Jane Austen, who spelt words in a variety of ways. The writer goes on to argue that the introduction of a standardized spelling system has done little more than become a way of 'torturing school children, judging Scrabble entries and filling in crosswords'. He makes his point clear to the reader through a pattern of three examples.

Notice how the writer uses the first person plural, 'we', to draw the reader into his side of the argument.

CORE TEXT

Earning our stripes

If tigers are to survive into the next century, it's high time we started paying for their upkeep, argues Julian Matthews

1   There can be few exceptions to match it. Nothing I had seen in Africa came close. My heart pounded softly above the rustle of the rushing branches sweeping across my seat on the elephant's lumbering grey viewing platform. I scanned the thick jungle ahead – I knew it was close.

2   All around the excited chatter of langur monkeys, the shrill of the peacock and the yelp of the chitral deer were music to my ears, but especially those of my *mahout. He knew that another good tip beckoned.

3   The tiger is a remarkable creature with a unique ability to attract attention, to instil fear, to create obsession, to help win elections, to boost economies, to fill wildlife charity coffers, to aid men's sex lives and to increase both the profits of legal and illegal companies. But it seems that the tiger is still incapable of saving itself.

4   There are now thought to be as few as 2,500 left in India, and only 7,000 across the rest of Asia. Yet from all the films, literature, reports and research that has been produced, little mention has ever been made of what I believe could be the tiger's real *trump card.

5   It is, in fact, one of the very reasons why most tiger reserves are still in existence: many people, like me, want to see them in the wild.

6   But it would appear that we are not paying for the privilege. Tens of millions of pounds, dollars and *rupees are spent every year by tourists in India to experience the extraordinary wildlife: a figure many times bigger than any wildlife agency has ever been able to raise. Sadly, only a very small percentage of this ever reaches the end product – India's wildlife and the local people who live in the vicinity of its influence.

7   The economic arguments of well-managed and sensitive nature tourism are well practised in parts of Africa, where millions of acres of colonial ranchland are being converted back to wilderness, saving a host of endangered species and reintroducing others once thought lost for ever. There, local communities have a real stakehold in the area's future, and schools and hospitals are funded directly from tourism revenue.

8   India has a steep uphill and bureaucratic struggle. Land that could conceivably be managed privately for nature tourism – those lands that may help preserve critical wilderness corridors or buffer zones – are under state control and cannot be released for what one might term 'conservation entrepreneurs'.

9   And not a single hotel or nature lodge next to Ranthambhore National Park in Rajasthan, pays a single rupee to the reserve into which every guest they host comes to visit.

10   But surely the park fees we pay go to the upkeep of the park? No. They pass across the desks of an estimated 30 departments before arriving in the coffers of the Department of Environment and Forests, the same department that allows the diversion of forest land for industry and commercial plantations.

11   Such red tape and negligence often ensures park budgets are not received for many months, leaving many rangers and anti-poaching teams without pay and highly demoralized. But time is running out for the tiger. It's time for action, time for us individually, and the unresponsive travel industry itself to use its purchasing power and influence to affect change.

12   We should pressurize the Indian government, the ground agents and hotel groups to be more accountable, and to seek ways to directly support cash-strapped parks working to protect Indian wildlife.

13   I bet not a single client going to see tigers in India would object to another £20 (or even more) being added to their holiday bill, if they knew it would help the tiger secure a wild future into the next millennium.

14   Alternatively, travel companies not wishing to indulge in the current mass hypocrisy should take those pretty pictures of tigers off their brochure covers.

The Guardian, July 17th 1999

*
mahout – elephant-driver
trump card – a resource that can be used to gain the final advantage
rupee – a monetary unit of India

Getting started

1 Look at the grid below and copy it out. It lists some of the techniques writers use to develop an argument. Find one example of each technique in the core text and comment on the effect it creates.

Technique	Example	Effect created
Facts		
Statistics		
Use of first person plural		
Repetition		
Pattern of three		
Rhetorical question		

2 Re-read paragraph 3 of the article. Why do you think the writer lists the qualities of the tiger? Why does he do it at this stage in the argument?

3 In some parts of the article, the writer uses language that is either emotive or dramatic to attack those who are threatening the survival of the tiger. Find three examples and comment on how effective they are in adding weight to the writer's argument.

Development

ACTIVITIES 4 Writers often use discourse connectives to structure a text and to signal a shift in the argument. Which discourse connectives does this writer use? (See page 96 to revise discourse connectives.)

5 The writer controls the pace of the text through his use of different sentence types. Re-read paragraph 1 and comment on how the sentence structures help to capture the reader's interest. Find two examples (in other paragraphs) where the writer varies the sentence types for effect and explain why you think he does it at those specific points. (See page 95 to revise sentence types.)

Extension

ACTIVITIES 6 The argument can be broken into approximately three stages (stage 1 paragraphs 1–5; stage 2 paragraphs 6–11; stage 3 paragraphs 12–14). What do you think are the writer's intentions at each stage? Explain how effective you think this structure is.

7 Overall, how effective do you find the writer's argument? Explore the writer's use of:
- a staged structure
- a variety of sentence types
- discourse connectives
- devices to involve the reader at different stages of the argument.

ADDITIONAL STUDY

English Paper 1, Section B, will include a writing task in which you are asked to develop an argument. To produce a successful piece of writing, you will need to consider using some or all of the techniques used in the extracts above.

ACTIVITY

Imagine that your head teacher and governors want to remove PE from the curriculum. Write a letter to them in which you argue against this idea.

Think about:

- form and layout
- audience – this will affect your tone and style
- purpose – to argue your point of view
- use of emotive and dramatic language
- use of facts and opinions to support your ideas.

Aim to write between 300 and 500 words, remembering to structure your ideas coherently and for effect.

Other topics that you may wish to develop arguments for or against are: GM foods, cosmetic surgery, designer labels and congestion charges in cities.

COMPARISON TEXT

Andrew Marvell was a lawyer from Hull who lived in the seventeenth century. 'To His Coy Mistress' is one of his most famous poems. The speaker is a young man who is trying to persuade a lady to become more intimate in their relationship. Being a lawyer, Marvell was skilled in using persuasive techniques. Try to identify them as you read the poem.

To His Coy Mistress

Had we but world enough, and time,
This coyness, Lady, were no crime.
We would sit down, and think which way
To walk, and pass our long love's day.
Thou by the Indian Ganges' side
Shouldst rubies find; I by the tide
Of Humber would complain. I would
Love you ten years before the flood:
And you should, if you please, refuse
Till the conversion of the Jews.
My vegetable love should grow
Vaster than empires, and more slow;
An hundred years should go to praise
Thine eyes, and on thy forehead gaze.
Two hundred to adore each breast:
But thirty thousand to the rest.
An age at least to every part,
And the last age should show your heart:
For, Lady, you deserve this state;
Nor would I love at lower rate.
  But at my back I always hear
Time's wingèd chariot hurrying near:

And yonder all before us lie
Deserts of vast eternity.
Thy beauty shall no more be found;
Nor, in thy marble vault, shall sound
My echoing song; then worms shall try
That long-preserved virginity:
And your quaint honour turn to dust;
And into ashes all my lust.
The grave's a fine and private place,
But none, I think, do there embrace.
  Now therefore, while the youthful hue
Sits on thy skin like morning glow,
And while thy willing soul transpires
At every pore with instant fires,
Now let us sport us while we may;
And now, like amorous birds of prey,
Rather at once our time devour,
Than languish in his slow-chapped power.
Let us roll all our strength, and all
Our sweetness, up into one ball:
And tear our pleasures with rough strife,
Through the iron gates of life.
Thus, though we cannot make our sun
Stand still, yet we will make him run.

ACTIVITY

Explore how both writers (Julian Matthews and Andrew Marvell) structure their arguments for effect. In your answer, consider:

◆ how each writer opens his argument (techniques used)
◆ how each one develops and builds up his point of view (techniques used)
◆ how each writer concludes his argument (techniques used)
◆ which writer you think uses structure to best effect.

FURTHER READING

The Penguin Book of Twentieth Century Protest, (Penguin, 1999)
Tatamkhulu Afrika, 'Nothing's Changed'. Reprinted in AQA Anthology Specification A
Tom Leonard, 'Unrelated Incidents'. Reprinted in AQA Anthology Specification A
John Agard, 'Half-Caste'. Reprinted in AQA Anthology Specification A
Jonathan Swift, A Modest Proposal and Other Satirical Works (Dover Thrift Editions, 1996)

1: Adapting forms for different readers and purposes

Introduction

When we write, we have to consider our audience (for whom we are writing) and our purpose (the reason we are writing). We also have to consider what form our writing should take. If we do not match our language and style to meet the needs of our audience, then our writing will fail to make an impression on our readers and it will fail to convey what we intend.

This section looks at extracts written on the same theme, but in different forms, for different audiences. An understanding of form will be important in your Original Writing for coursework (English) and for the writing sections of English Papers 1 and 2.

Read the following three extracts, all of which focus on Queen Elizabeth 1. One was written for young children, one for teenagers and one for adults.

Extract 1
Elizabeth faced many dangers. When she was 29 she almost died of smallpox. Her advisers begged her to marry and have a child. They wanted her to have an heir.

From *Queen Elizabeth I* by Rachael Bell

Extract 2
Elizabeth I – Frizzie Lizzie
Claim to fame – Elizabeth never married but she had a few close shaves (No, not on her head, you fool). There are some men she came close to marrying several times. The first victim was Robert Dudley . . .

From *Cruel Kings and Mean Queens* by Terry Deary

Extract 3
Everyone assumed that Elizabeth would soon marry and mother an heir to the throne, so the question of the succession was regarded as secondary to the Queen's marriage. As a Princess, there had been no shortage of candidates from the Continent . . .

From *The Life and Times of Elizabeth I* by Neville Williams

Notice how the form of each extract is different to meet the needs of a different audience. Extract 1 is clearly aimed at young children as it is written in simple sentences with basic vocabulary. Extract 2 is more informal with use of colloquial language, for example, 'flings', 'close shaves' and the light-hearted rhyme 'Frizzie Lizzie'. The chatty nature of the text comes through in the aside, which addresses the teenage audience directly: 'No, not on her head, you fool'. The sentences are still simple and easy to follow. Extract 3 is aimed at a more advanced, adult reader. The vocabulary is more sophisticated, including words such as 'assumed', 'succession', 'secondary' and 'candidates'. The sentences are complex with the use of main and subordinate clauses to carry more detailed information. (See page 95 for revision of sentence types.)

KEY TERM	**Form** – the style, shape and structure

CORE TEXTS

The Anglo-Saxon poem 'Beowulf' is one of the most famous stories in the world. It was written in Old English, and it tells of the hero Beowulf, his quest against the monster Grendel, and his fated death as a defender of his people. The story has been reworked and translated many times. The following extracts all recount the episode in which the monster, Grendel, attacks the Great Hall.

Extract 1

Grendel waited hidden among the trees until the Great Hall had fallen silent and the last revellers had wandered to their homes, sleepy and exhausted by the feasting. The king had left his favourite warriors to guard the Hall, but because there was peace in the land, they did not take their guard-duty seriously. They fell asleep, and did not hear Grendel croaking his terrible song as he moved out from the shadows towards them:

Sweet human meat's the best to eat,
And human bones the best to grind,
Human blood will flow again
And cold terror haunt the human mind.

A century of sleep had whetted Grendel's appetite. He crashed into the Great Hall and surprised the sleeping warriors. He plucked off their limbs as if they were petals. Blood filled the Great Hall. It dripped from the rafters and flowed out into the moonlight. Grendel ate his fill, then gathering into his powerful arms the warriors he could not eat, the demon slouched back off to his dwelling-place in the fetid marshland pools.

From *Beowulf* by Brian Patten

Extract 2

In the darkest hour of the spring night Grendel came to Heorot as he had come so many times before, up from his lair and over the high moors, through the mists that seemed to travel with him under the pale moon: Grendel the Night-Striker, the Death-Shadow. He came to the foreporch and snuffed about it, and smelled the man-smell, and found that the door which had stood unlatched for him so long was barred and bolted. Snarling in rage that any man should dare attempt to keep him out, he set the flat of his talon-tipped hands against the timbers and burst them in.

Dark as it was, the hall seemed to fill with a monstrous shadow at his coming; a shadow in which Beowulf, half springing up, then holding himself in frozen stillness, could make out no shape nor clear outline save two eyes filled with a wavering greenish flame.

The ghastly corpse-light of his own eyes showed Grendel the shapes of men as it seemed sleeping and he did not notice among them one who leaned up on his elbow. Laughing in his throat, he reached out and grabbed young Hondscio who lay nearest to him, and almost before his victim had time to cry out, tore him limb from limb and drank the warm blood. Then, while the young warrior's dying shriek still hung upon the air, he reached for another. But this time his hand was met and seized in a grasp such as he had never felt before; a grasp that had in it the strength of thirty men. And for the first time he who had brought fear to so many caught the taste of it himself, knowing that at last he had met his match and maybe his master.

Beowulf leapt from the sleeping-bench and grappled him in the darkness; and terror broke over Grendel in full force, the terror of a wild animal trapped; so that he thought no more of his hunting but only breaking the terrible hold upon his arm and flying back into the night and the wilderness, and he howled and bellowed as he struggled for his freedom. Beowulf set his teeth and summoned all his strength and tightened his grip until the sinews cracked; and locked together they reeled and staggered up and down the great hall. Trestles and sleeping-benches went over with crash on crash as they strained this way and that, trampling even through the last red embers of the dying fire; and the very walls seemed to groan and shudder as though the stout timbers would burst apart. And all the while Grendel snarled and shrieked and Beowulf fought in silence save for his gasping breaths.

From *Beowulf: Dragonslayer* by Rosemary Sutcliff

Extract 3

In off the moors, down through the mist-bands
God-cursed Grendel came greedily loping.
The bane of the race of men roamed forth,
hunting for prey in the high hall.
Under the cloud-murk he moved towards it
until it shone above him, a sheer keep
of fortified gold. Nor was that the first time
he had scouted the grounds of Hrothgar's dwelling –
although never in his life, before or since,
did he find harder fortune or hall-defenders.
Spurned and joyless, he journeyed on ahead
and arrived at the bawn. The iron-braced door
turned on its hinge when his hands touched it.
Then his rage boiled over, he ripped open
the mouth of the building, maddening for blood,
pacing the length of the patterned floor
with his loathsome tread, while a baleful light,
flame more than light, flared from his eyes.
He saw many men in the mansion, sleeping,
a ranked company of kinsmen and warriors
quartered together. And his glee was demonic,
picturing the mayhem: before morning
he would rip life from limb and devour them,
feed on their flesh; but his fate that night
was due to change, his days of ravening
had come to an end.

Mighty and canny,
Hygelac's kinsman was keenly watching
for the first move the monster would make.
Nor did the creature keep him waiting
but struck suddenly and started in;
he grabbed and mauled a man on his bench,
bit into his bone-lappings, bolted down his blood
and gorged on him in lumps, leaving his body
utterly lifeless, eaten up
hand and foot. Venturing closer,
his talon was raised to attack Beowulf
where he lay on the bed, he was bearing in
with open claw when the alert hero's
comeback and armlock forestalled him utterly.
The captain of evil discovered himself
in a handgrip harder than anything
he had ever encountered in any man
on the face of the earth. Every bone in his body
quailed and recoiled, but he could not escape.
He was desperate to flee to his den and hide
with the devil's litter, for in all his days
he had never been clamped or cornered like this.

From *Beowulf* by Seamus Heaney

Getting started

ACTIVITIES

1 Look at the form of extracts 1 to 3. Assign an audience and purpose to each text and give a couple of examples of text features that helped you decide.

2 Look at extract 1. Explore the techniques used to tailor the text to its audience by copying and completing the grid below.

Technique	Example	How effective is it?
Use of simple sentences		
Rhyme		
Simple vocabulary		
Vivid description		
Basic use of figurative language		

3 The original, Old English manuscript of *Beowulf*, was written in verse, like the Heaney extract. Why do you think the other writers (Brian Patten and Rosemary Sutcliff) chose to write in prose?

Development

ACTIVITIES 4 Re-read extract 2. What techniques has the writer used to meet the needs of her readers? Copy and complete the grid below, adding more techniques that you can identify.

Technique	Example	How effective is it?
Sentence types		
Use of atmospheric language		
Use of verbs to build tension		
Use of sound words		
Descriptive language		

5 How and why does the writer build up the tension and suspense in extract 2? Look back at question 3 to help you.

6 Compare and contrast extracts 1 and 2. What similarities and differences do you notice in how each has been written to meet the needs of its audience?

Extension

ACTIVITIES 7 Re-read extract 3 by Seamus Heaney. Complete the chart below to explore the devices and techniques he uses. Add other techniques that you can identify.

Technique	Example	How effective is it?
Sentence lengths		
Use of verbs to build drama		
Complex description		
Poetic devices		

8 The form of the Heaney extract is more controlled, tighter and condensed than the other two extracts. Do you think it works well as poetry after having read the two prose versions? What advantages are there in writing it as verse? Explain your thoughts in a few paragraphs.

ADDITIONAL STUDY

ACTIVITY   Look at all three extracts. Which one do you feel meets the needs of its audience and fulfils its purpose best? Give reasons for your answer (refer back to questions 2, 4 and 7).

COMPARISON TEXT

ACTIVITY   Find a piece of text (preferably poetry or literary prose) that you have enjoyed reading. It can be for any audience. Rework it for two different audiences. Refer back to the questions on the Beowulf texts to remind yourself of the techniques that each writer employed to suit his or her target audience.

When you have produced your two new versions, write an analysis of the changes that you have made to the form. This might focus on:

◆ the tone of the narrative voice (e.g. chatty, formal)
◆ sentence types and lengths
◆ use of language (e.g. descriptive, figurative)
◆ level of vocabulary.

FURTHER READING

Biographies that are aimed at specific audiences (a mixture of celebrity, sports, political, historical and literary biographies)
Classic literature in various forms, including: original form; abridged version; cartoon version (book or film). *A Christmas Carol* by Charles Dickens, for example, is available in many different forms (including *The Muppets Christmas Carol*).

2: EFFECTS OF WRITER'S CHOICE OF FORM

INTRODUCTION

Have you ever wondered why, as a small child, you found it easy to
learn nursery rhymes and why you can still recite many of them? It is
probably due to the regular rhyme scheme (often rhyming couplets –
a, a, b, b), the metre (beat and pace in each line) and the simple
subject matter. Writers use different forms to suit the content of their
work. For example, a haiku is a short pithy form used to convey a
single image or moment. Free verse is a loose form without rhyme or
beat, often used to convey meandering thoughts and images. This unit
looks at how writers choose different forms for different effects.

I wanna be yours
by John Cooper Clarke

let me be your vacuum cleaner
breathing in your dust
let me be your ford cortina
i will never rust
if you like your coffee hot
let me be your coffee pot
you call the shots
i wanna be yours
let me be your raincoat
for those frequent rainy days
let me be your dreamboat
when you wanna sail away
let me be your teddy bear
take me with you anywhere

i don't care
i wanna be yours
let me be your electric meter
i will not run out
let me be the electric heater
you get cold without
let me be your setting lotion
hold your hair with deep devotion
deep as the deep atlantic ocean
that's how deep is my emotion
deep deep deep deep de deep deep
i don't wanna be hers
i wanna be yours

ACTIVITY In this poem, John Cooper Clarke is expressing his love for someone.
In a small group, explore why he might have used this form. How does
it add to our understanding of his emotion? Look in particular at:

♦ rhyme and the patterned rhythm (See page 90 for revision of metre)
♦ repetition
♦ punctuation (and the speed at which you are forced to read the poem)
♦ the lack of capital letters
♦ similarities to the images and diction used in popular love songs.

CORE TEXT

The following poem was written to express anger about low-flying planes that spoil the peace and tranquillity of the Welsh countryside.

No Hands
by Gillian Clarke

War-planes have been at it all day long
shaking the world, strung air
humming like pianos when children bang the keys

over and over, willow warbler song
and jet planes; lads high on speed up there   5
in a mindless thrum; down here a brake of trees
churns to a rolling wave and there's no let
in the after-quiver along air-waves struck
by silly boys who think they strum guitars,

who skim the fields like surfboards over crests   10
of hedges, where a tractor swims in a green wake
of grass dust tossed to dry under sun and stars:

boy scaring boy off the face of his own land,
all do and dare, and look at me, no hands.

Getting started

ACTIVITIES 1 Work out the rhyme scheme of the poem (using letters of the alphabet). What do you notice about the scansion (rhythm structure, see page 90)? Does it vary? If so, for what effect?

2 You should have noticed that lines 10, 11 and 12 do not exactly rhyme with lines 7, 8 and 9. However, there are similarities in the final words: the vowel sounds in 'let' and 'crests' are the same (assonance); 'struck' and 'wake' are near rhymes, with the same final consonant sounds. Why do you think the poet uses this technique of 'near misses' rather than exact rhyme, as she does in the rest of the poem?

Development

ACTIVITIES
3 In the final two lines (which almost form a rhyming couplet, although one ending is singular and the other plural) the style is like a nursery rhyme. Why do you think the poet ended the poem in this way?

4 The poet uses a technique called enjambement. This means that there is no punctuation at the end of each line, so the lines run on. (The alternative technique is end-stopping, where punctuation at the end of a line gives a natural pause, like at the end of a sentence.) Read the poem through to yourself again, but pause at the end of each line. Then read it again pausing only when you reach a form of punctuation. What do you notice about using this technique? Why do you think Gillian Clarke uses it?

Extension

ACTIVITIES
5 The form of the poem is almost the same as a sonnet. (Remember that a sonnet is a short lyric poem of 14 lines, which has one of several traditional rhyme schemes. It is usually written in the first person and is concerned with the speaker's emotions.) Why do you think the poet chose to use a modified sonnet form to convey her feelings?

6 Most sonnets are written in iambic pentameter (five pairs of stressed/unstressed beats per line). Look at the metre of a few lines e.g. lines 3 and 4 in the poem. What do you notice about the metre? Why might the poet have used it in this way?

7 This poem is all one sentence, with a colon, a semicolon and a series of commas. What effect does this have?

ADDITIONAL STUDY

ACTIVITY
How effective do you find Gillian Clarke's use of form in 'No Hands' in conveying her message to the reader?

Think about:

◆ her use of rhythm, rhyme and assonance for effect
◆ the effect of using enjambement
◆ the use of a mock sonnet form.

COMPARISON TEXT

ACTIVITY Compare how Gillian Clarke and one other poet use form to contribute to their subject matter. Suitable comparative poems in your AQA *Anthology* might be:

'Limbo' by Edward Kamau Braithwaite
'Two Scavengers in a Truck' by Lawrence Ferlinghetti
'Unrelated Incidents' by Tom Leonard
'Half-Caste' by John Agard
'On my first Sonne' by Ben Jonson
'Sonnet 130' by William Shakespeare.

FURTHER READING

Poems by E.E. Cummings in *The Faber Book of Modern Verse*, 4th ed.
   Revd Peter Porter (Faber and Faber, 1982)
Ted Hughes *Season Songs* (Faber and Faber, 1985)
Benjamin Zephaniah, *The Dread Affair: Collected Poems* (Arena, 1985)

3: Spoken versus written form

Introduction

In conversation, most of what we say is spontaneous and we often adjust our ideas while we are talking. We often hesitate, to give us time to think, and use 'fillers', such as 'like' and 'you know'. These fillers have little meaning, but they generally invite our listeners to agree with what we are saying. We tend to speak in long sentences that can change direction; we repeat ideas or points; we use informal phrases and vocabulary, dialect and slang. However, when we write, our expressions tend to be more formal. We use controlled sentence structures; Standard English; more carefully selected vocabulary, and less dialect. Writing rarely contains hesitations and fillers, unless it is the speech of a character in a novel or playscript.

This section examines some of the differences between spoken and written language.

Read these two versions of the same account:

Spoken version
Them lads is going to get in bother soon. They's real rum 'uns, like. I were on me way t'shop t'other day when one of 'em, erm, shouted somat rude.

Written version
Those boys are going to be in trouble soon. Some of them are really cheeky. The other day, I was on my way to the shop when of one them shouted something rude at me.

ACTIVITY Copy and complete the grid on the next page to draw out the differences between the spoken and written extracts. Add any additional features that you can identify in the extracts.

Which version is the easiest to follow? Explain why.

Feature	Spoken (dialectical)	Written (Standard English)
Pronoun usage		
Informal language		
Subject/verb agreement		
Dialect		
Fillers		
Hesitations		

CORE TEXT

The following extracts are two versions of the same account – one spoken and one written. The narrator is from Bolton, Lancashire.

A

Spoken version (from a tape transcript)

One day we were – me and an elderly fellow who worked for the joiner chappy that I worked for – were passing by a certain chimney in Bolton that's very large and close to the pavement. And Mr Faulkner and his men were busily engaged on renovating the thing. And – God, you know – I can see it now, as a kid you know – I'd be about fifteen and the platform round the top looked like it were made out of lollypop sticks, you know, it were so far away and the rungs in the ladders like – the sides of the ladders looked like matchsticks you know, they were so . . . I think it were eighteen ladders high this chimney, you know, that's a lot a ladders you know, one piled on top o' t'other . . . Anyway I said to the joiner fellow, you know, I said, 'I'd like climb up there, you know,' and he said, 'You'll never b . . . . get up there,' like, you know, sort of thing. The thing is that he insulted me, you know. I knew I could get up that chimney. And he said that I'd never do it and he bet me ten bob.

Anyway the thing is we were in this park the other side of Bolton mending the old veterans' hut. And I'm rooting in this box and I found a union jack – b . . . . big union jack, and one them like four foot six by about seven foot, you see and I thought, 'This is it,' you know, 'I'm going to get this flag and I'm going to climb up this chimney and tie it to the lightning conductor,' you see. So I'm coming home on the bus that night with a flag stuffed up inside me jumper, and there's a fellow sat on – you know – 'Hello Fred,' like – sat on same seat you see. And he enquired about the unusual bulkiness of me shirt you see. And being like all little lads do full of bravado you know, I mean I've never been good at keeping secrets, I've gotta tell him what I were going to do with this b . . . . union jack, you see. And he said, 'We've got a union jack like that. I'll give you ours in t'morning. Put two up!'

Everything went like clockwork, you know, until the b . . . . horror of it sticks in me mind even now, you know. Them boards – they were twenty foot long the boards at the top. Maybe you've never experienced walking on a plank twenty feet long, that's supported at about fifteen foot centres: it sort of bends – you know like. As you put one foot on one plank that goes down and the other one lifts up and it's like walking on bloody cloud. And it were quite fantastic . . . I mean I'd never been that high in me life – off the floor – before, under me own steam. I mean, I'm only fifteen years old and it's dark and I can see all the road lights twinkling all down below – a lot less than what there are now. Anyway I tied the flags to the lightning conductors and beat a hasty retreat.

B

Written version

One day, an elderly man and myself, who were both working for a joiner, were passing by a chimney in Bolton which is very large and stands close to the pavement. Mr Faulkner and his men were busily engaged in renovating it. It had stood there for years as I remember it when I was a boy of 15. It had a platform around the top which looked as though it had been made from lollipop sticks and the ladder which went up the chimney looked like a line of matchsticks. It was a very tall chimney, roughly the size of eighteen ladders stacked on top of each other. I said to the joiner that I would like to climb up the chimney but he replied that I'd never manage it as it was so high. I was rather annoyed at his response as I felt that I could climb up there. He bet me ten shillings that I could not reach the top.

We were in a park at the other side of Bolton repairing the old veterans' hut. Whilst searching in a box, I found an enormous Union Jack flag (about four feet six by seven feet). It struck me that I could take the flag, climb to the top of the chimney and attach it to the lightning conductor. Later, whilst on my way home on the bus, with the flag lodged up my jumper, I met Fred, sitting close by. He enquired about the unusual bulkiness of my shirt. Being a typical boy, full of bravado, and not very good at keeping secrets, I told him what I intended to do with the flag. He said that he too had a Union Jack flag and that I could have his and fly two the next morning.

Everything went to plan, I remember it so clearly. There were twenty-foot boards at the top of the chimney. I remember that it was like walking on a long plank that bent at various points and made it feel like you were walking on a cloud, moving up and down haphazardly. It was fantastic . . . I had never experienced anything like it before. I was only fifteen years old; it was dark and I could only see the street lights twinkling below, though they were not as bright as they are today. I tied the flags to the lightning conductors and retreated hastily.

Getting started

ACTIVITIES

1 In extract A, find examples of where the speaker uses informal words and phrases. What effect do these have on the reader/listener? What type of relationship does it establish, or assume, between the speaker and listener?

2 In conversation, our thoughts become speech very quickly and we do not always think ahead. Sometimes we alter our train of thought mid-sentence. Look at where the speaker does this. Does it confuse the reader/listener or is it still clear to follow?

3 When we read spoken English, what disadvantages do we have that a face-to-face listener does not? Think about visual means of communication during a conversation.

Development

ACTIVITIES

4 In several places in extract A, the speaker uses his own dialect. Find two examples of this. Why is it acceptable in speech but inadvisable in written English?

5 The speaker does not always follow the rules of subject/verb agreement. Find at least one example of this. Why do you think we often break this rule in speech but usually follow it in writing?

Extension

6 In speech we often vary our use of pronouns. Where does the speaker do this in extract A? Why is it acceptable in speech?

7 At certain points the speaker swears (only the initial letters of swear words are printed here). What effect do you think the speaker is hoping to achieve by this? What concept or emotion is he trying to convey? Why would this not be acceptable in a written version?

8 Compare the original spoken text with the written version. What differences do you notice in:
 ◆ tone   ◆ formality   ◆ meaning
 ◆ length   ◆ any other areas that you can identify?

ADDITIONAL STUDY/COMPARISON TEXTS

ACTIVITY   Select one of the following activities.

1 Record an edition of a news programme (BBC, ITV, Channel 4, 5, SKY, etc.). Examine how language varies in the programme by focusing on:

 ◆ the differences in style and formality between presenter and the public that speak (in interviews)
 ◆ the differences in rehearsed or scripted speech and spontaneous speech.

2 Find a short written text which tells a story (it might be a fairytale, an urban myth or even a long joke). Give the written version to a range of people, preferably of different ages and if possible, from different regional backgrounds. Ask them to read the story. Then, with their permission, use a tape recorder to record them retelling the story in their own words, without reference to the written version. Transcribe your recordings and compare the spoken and written versions of the story. Consider:

 ◆ Are parts of the written version missed out/added in the spoken versions?
 ◆ Is the same vocabulary and phrasing used?
 ◆ Which versions are most formal/informal?
 ◆ How do sentence structures vary?
 ◆ Where can you identify Standard English and dialect?
 ◆ In which versions are the speaker's train of thought clearest? Do any of them change direction mid-sentence?
 ◆ Are the spoken or written versions longest?

1: LANGUAGE AS CHARACTERISTIC OF PERIOD AND WRITER

INTRODUCTION

Most writers have a distinct style. This style is a reflection of both the period in which the writer lives and the writer's individuality. For example, Shakespeare's writing is in many ways typical of the Elizabethan era, in that it focuses on kings, queens and high-ranking people (Shakespeare wrote for Elizabeth I and James I); it deals with much-debated moral issues of the time, such as family quarrels; love; the personal and the private being. Shakespeare's individuality as a writer is apparent in his use of highly crafted imagery within tightly structured iambic pentameter. (See page 90 for revision of metre.)

In your GCSE coursework for English Literature, you will need to show an understanding of the social, cultural and historical context of texts. This means that you will be expected to identify language and ideas in the texts that are characteristic of the writer and the period in which they lived.

The first two extracts that we are going to look at are from the Victorian period. Some of the main features of the Victorian period (1837–1901) were:

- rapid change and progress (in education, industry, agriculture, transport and communication)
- the mass exodus of village people moving to cities and towns to find work in factories and mills
- suffering through poor health, in particular sanitation problems, inadequate housing, pollution and overcrowding in cities.

As well as reflecting these social and economic issues, many Victorian novels shared other characteristics:

- they were often episodic because the novels were published in parts, for magazines
- each episode (which later became a chapter) usually ended with the tension built up to a climax (like in a modern soap opera)
- characters were often crude and caricatured; a strong focus on heroes and villains
- there was a focus on detail and texture in description (heavy use of imagery)
- writers often wrote in a dense style, using many complex sentences.

Read the extract below, which describes a Victorian teacher. (Compulsory education was just being introduced when Dickens wrote this.)

The scene was a plain, bare, monotonous vault of a school room, and the speaker's square forefinger emphasized his observations by underscoring every sentence with a line on the schoolmaster's sleeve. The emphasis was helped by the speaker's square wall of a forehead, which had his eyebrows for its base, while his eyes found commodious cellarage in two dark caves, overshadowed by the wall. The emphasis was helped by the speaker's mouth, which was wide, thin, and hard set. The emphasis was helped by the speaker's voice, which was inflexible, dry, and dictatorial. The emphasis was helped by the speaker's hair, which bristled on the skirts of his bald head, a plantation of firs to keep the wind from its shining surface, all covered with knobs, like the crust of a plum pie, as if the head had scarcely warehouse-room for the hard facts stored inside. The speaker's obstinate carriage, square coat, square legs, square shoulders, – nay, his very neckcloth, trained to take him by the throat with an unaccommodating grasp, like a stubborn fact, as it was, – all helped the emphasis.

From *Hard Times* by Charles Dickens

This passage demonstrates typical features of Dickens's style of writing:

◆ use of repetition
◆ use of contrast to give texture to the narrative
◆ long complex sentences allowing detailed description
◆ abundant use of adjectives
◆ figurative language (metaphor, simile)
◆ grotesque and satirical caricatures
◆ exaggeration to get a point across and create comedy or pass social comment.

CORE TEXT

This next passage is the opening of another novel by Charles Dickens.

1 London. Michaelmas Term lately over, and the Lord Chancellor sitting in Lincoln's Inn Hall. Implacable November weather. As much mud in the streets, as if the waters had but newly retired from the face of the earth, and it would not be wonderful to meet a Megalosaurus, forty feet long or so, waddling like an elephantine lizard up Holborn-Hill. Smoke lowering down from chimney-pots, making a soft black drizzle, with flakes of soot

in it as big as full-grown snow-flakes—gone into mourning, one might imagine, for the death of the sun. Dogs, undistinguishable in mire. Horses, scarcely better; splashed to their very blinkers. Foot passengers, jostling one another's umbrellas, in a general infection of ill-temper, and losing their foot-hold at street-corners, where tens of thousands of other foot passengers have been slipping and sliding since the day broke (if the day ever broke), adding new deposits to the crust upon crust of mud, sticking at those points tenaciously to the pavement, and accumulating at compound interest.

2   Fog everywhere. Fog up the river, where it flows among green *aits and meadows; fog down the river, where it rolls defied among the tiers of shipping, and the waterside pollutions of a great (and dirty) city. Fog on the Essex marshes, fog on the Kentish heights. Fog creeping into the *cabooses of *collier-brigs; fog lying out on the yards and hovering in the rigging of great ships; fog drooping on the gunwales of barges and small boats. Fog in the eyes and throats of ancient Greenwich pensioners, wheezing by the firesides of their wards; fog in the stem and bowl of the afternoon pipe of the wrathful skipper, down in his close cabin; fog cruelly pinching the toes and fingers of his shivering little 'prentice boy on deck. Chance people on the bridges peeping over the parapets into a *nether sky of fog, with fog all round them, as if they were up in a balloon, and hanging in the misty clouds.

3   Gas looming through the fog in divers places in the streets, much as the sun may, from the spongey fields, be seen to loom by husbandman and ploughboy. Most of the shops lighted two hours before their time—as the gas seems to know, for it has a haggard and unwilling look.

4   The raw afternoon is rawest, and the dense fog is densest, and the muddy streets are muddiest, near that leaden-headed old obstruction, appropriate ornament for the threshold of a leaden-headed old corporation: Temple Bar. And hard by Temple Bar, in Lincoln's Inn Hall, at the very heart of the fog, sits the Lord High Chancellor in his High Court of Chancery.

5   Never can there come fog too thick, never can there come mud and mire too deep, to assort with the groping and floundering condition which this High Court of Chancery, most pestilent of hoary sinners, holds, this day, in the sight of heaven and earth.

*
aits – small isles in a river
cabooses – cook rooms on a ship's deck
collier-brigs – sea vessels carrying coal
nether – low or lower

From *Bleak House* by Charles Dickens

Getting started

1 Dickens uses repetition of certain words, phrases and structures. Find examples of repetition and suggest why he uses this technique. What might he be trying to suggest about his own times?

2 In paragraph 2, Dickens makes the fog seem sinister. How does he do this? Find examples.

3 Look at paragraph 2 again. Find examples of the verbs that Dickens uses to describe the fog and to show how people are reacting to it. What do you notice about the verbs? What do they suggest about the fog?

Development

4 Dickens uses figurative language to build up the scene for the reader. Find a few examples where he uses this technique and explore how effective they are.

5 Look at paragraphs 1 and 2 again. Notice how Dickens varies his sentence lengths. Count the number of words in each sentence and then suggest reasons why he varies the lengths. What effect might he have wanted to create?

6 In places, Dickens exaggerates ideas for effect. Find one example and explore what effect you think he wanted to create. How might this be used to pass social comment?

Extension

7 Re-read the first three sentences in the opening paragraph. Here Dickens uses broken sentence structures for effect. What effect? How might this opening attract a Victorian reader?

8 Re-read paragraphs 3 and 4. Dickens implies that there is corruption in the judicial system through his use of language. For example: 'leaden-headed old obstruction' suggests it is a harsh system with out-of-date rules that are extreme and unlikely to alter for the better. Select other examples of where he uses language to suggest corruption and comment on the effectiveness of these.

9 How can you tell that this text was written in the nineteenth century? Think about Dickens's use of:

♦ sentence structures and lengths
♦ language and vocabulary
♦ various ways of building up detail for the reader
♦ specific references to time and place.

ADDITIONAL STUDY

ACTIVITY This is a detailed and complex text. Re-write it for a young reader (between ages 8 and10). Think about:

- using simple and compound sentences rather than complex ones
- using shorter sentences
- simplifying vocabulary and imagery
- making the author's feelings more explicit (less subtle)
- keeping the overall atmosphere of the scene the same.

COMPARISON TEXT

ACTIVITY One of the main themes of twentieth-century literature was war and destruction: many writers saw it as an age of horror and social fragmentation. Some writers wrote in forms that reflected this feeling of violence and dislocation, often using blunt, incomplete sentences with a very direct first-person narrative.

FRED

An hour after murdering my mother I was in Soho. That was where it began. In the dress shop in Greek Street. In the changing room. I was on the run. A criminal. I saw myself: one of those men, framed in black, on a police poster; hollow-eyed, wild-haired, staring. I slowed my pace, tried to stop shaking. Tried to make myself invisible: dug my hands into my jacket pockets and slouched, my cap pulled low and my eyes swivelling from side to side to spot any approaching trouble.

I'd always had a gift for inventing stories. I shuffled them like a pack of cards in my head. When I made them up I believed they were true. Other people called them lies or excuses. I wondered what story to tell when I was caught, hauled to the cells. I couldn't imagine a story that would explain away my guilt. I was a killer. That was a fact.

In half an hour's time I was due to meet Martin outside the cinema in Wardour Street . . . After the film Martin and I would go to a coffee-bar and talk. I'd try to tell him about the blood. I might ask him to help me to decide what to do.

I loafed along Old Compton Street to spin away the time. I prowled in and out of Italian grocery shops, checked the pyramids of strawberry tarts in the patisseries' windows, surveyed the other strollers – the ones like myself who just looked, and the ones who preened, who offered themselves in my furtive gaze. A woman in silver brocade and stilettos. A girl in white plastic boots, white plastic mini-dress with cut-out holes. A slender boy, hair greased and quaffed, in drainpipes and brothel creepers. An old woman in a jade-green turban and a blue catsuit.

It began to rain. Fierce pellets of water hit the back of my neck and dripped inside my collar. I quickened my pace. To guilt I added chill misery. My jacket was no protection against the suddenly cool air, the wind which had sprung up. Raindrops slid down my eyelids and nose. I ducked around the street corner and into the nearest doorway, shivering.

From *Flesh and Blood* by Michèle Roberts

ACTIVITY

Examine how Dickens and Roberts use language, structure and style that are characteristic of the period in which they are writing.

FURTHER READING

Other Victorian novels:

Charles Dickens: *Bleak House*; *David Copperfield*; *A Tale of Two Cities*; *Hard Times* (all published in the Oxford World's Classics series, OUP, latest editions 1998, except *A Tale of Two Cities*, 1999)

Arthur Conan Doyle: A variety of titles published by OUP in the series, The Oxford Sherlock Holmes

George Eliot: *Middlemarch*; *Silas Marner*; *Adam Bede* (all published in the Oxford World's Classics series, OUP, latest editions 1998)

Elizabeth Gaskell, *North and South* (Oxford World's Classics, OUP, 1998)

Modern novels:

E. Annie Proulx, *The Shipping News* (Fourth Estate, 2002)

James Joyce, *Ulysses* (Oxford World's Classics, OUP, 1998)

2: LANGUAGE VARIATION AND CHANGE

INTRODUCTION

Have you ever wondered what our ancestors would think if we described a game as 'wicked' or if we sent them a message written 'CUL8R'? They would probably think the game was immoral and be completely baffled by the message! This is because language changes. It changes because people and society change. Invaders, such as the Romans, Vikings and Normans, brought new words into the English language. For example, 'street' comes from the Latin *strata*; 'husband', 'egg' and 'dale' are Old Norse words; 'court', 'power' and 'paint' are from Norman French words.

In more recent times, new inventions brought new words into the language, e.g. 'bicycle', 'television', 'skateboard'. Some inventions were named after their inventors, e.g. 'biro', 'morse' and 'hoover'. As technology develops, we adapt our language to communicate quickly and efficiently. Emails and text messages use a shortened form of English. Each generation invents its own slang and new colloquial forms. Dictionaries help to standardize language and spelling, but they need constant updating to include new words and explain new meanings of old words.

There are different varieties of English. For example, when America became independent in 1776, the American people wanted a language distinct from British English. A book called *The American Spelling Book* encouraged Americans to change their language, for example, spelling words ending in '-our', '-or', and reversing '-re' to '-er' (which is why Americans spell 'color' and 'center' like this). More people in the world now speak American English than British English.

In this section, we are going to look at many aspects of language change over time, including vocabulary, spellings, word order and verbs forms.

Look at this short passage from a Middle English poem, written in the fourteenth century.

> She wolde wepe, if that she saugh a mous
> Kaught in a trappe, if it were deed or bledde.
> Of smale houndes hadde she that she fedde
> With rosted flesh, or milk and *wastel-breed.
> But soore wepte she if oon of hem were deed…
>
> *wastel-breed – fine white bread

From the Prologue to *The Canterbury Tales* by Geoffrey Chaucer

Most of the words are recognizable today, even though spellings have altered. The word order is different from modern English (although it may have been manipulated slightly to fit the poem format). For example, 'Of smale houndes hadde she that she fedde', would now be: 'She had some small dogs that she fed'. Notice that the verb and subject reverse today, 'hadde she' becomes 'she had'. In the final line, look at the order of the adverb and verb, 'soore wepte'. How would we express this today? The word 'flesh' in Middle English was commonly used to describe 'meat'. This might have developed from the Germanic word 'fleisch' which means 'meat'. What other differences between Middle and modern English can you find?

CORE TEXT

The next extract is part of a letter written by Margaret Paston to her husband, John, in the fifteenth century.

The character þ is called 'thorn' and represents the sound 'th'. The thorn has long not been in use in English, but it existed in Chaucer's time and persisted even later in the dialects of the North and the Midlands of England. The thorn occurs frequently in the letters of the Pastons, a well-to-do family from Norfolk.

> Right wurshippfull hosbond, I recommand me to yow, praying yow to wete [*know*] that þe [*the*] man of Knapton þat owyth yow mony sent me this weke xxxix s. viij d.; and as for þe remenant of þe mony, he hath promysid to bring itt at Wytsontyd. And as for þe prest [*priest*], Howardys sone, he yede to Canbryge [*Cambridge*] þe last weke and he shall nomore come hom tyll itt be mydsomer, and therfore I myght not do yowr erunde. As for tydyngys, þe Quene come in-to þis town on Tewysday last past after none and abode here tyll itt was Thursday iij after none, and she sent after my cosyn Elysabeth Clere be Sharynborn to come to here. And she durst not dysabey here commandment, and come to here. . . .
>
> . . . The blissid Trinyté have yow in his kepyng. Wretyn at Norwych on þe Fryday next before Seynt George.
>
> Be yowrys, M. Paston.

Getting started

ACTIVITIES

1 Margaret wrote this letter to her husband over 500 years ago. Although the English language has changed over that time, there are still enough similarities for modern readers to understand the letter. Copy and complete the grid below to analyze how Margaret's English was different from/the same as modern English. Fill in two or three examples for each column.

Words that are no longer used	Words with different spelling	Words that are exactly the same

2 Language changes to mirror other changes in society, for example changes in fashion, beliefs, education and material goods. Margaret talks about money that her husband is owed by the man of Knapton. She mentions a sum that he has sent her. Can you work out what it is? Why is it not written in £ (pounds) and p (pence)? What would we use instead of roman numerals today?

Development

ACTIVITIES

3 Language reflects the way people live and measure their time. Time and dates are mentioned frequently in this extract. List those mentioned – there are days of the week, a saint's day, a religious period, a seasonal time and also times of the day. How are these references different from the language we would use to describe specific times today?

4 In some sentences the word order is different from modern English. Find a couple of examples and compare them with how we would write them today. Which words (in terms of their word class, see page 91) seem to be used in a different sequence from the way we would use them today?

Extension

ACTIVITIES

5 Most of the letter is written informally. Identify examples of where the language seems chatty and informal. Are these words and expressions close to modern English?

6 Now identify more formal parts of the letter. Look in particular at the opening and ending. How do you think the language reflects social and religious beliefs of the time?

ADDITIONAL STUDY

ACTIVITY Update the letter by reworking it in modern English. Write a short analysis of the changes that you made in terms of:

- ◆ modernizing vocabulary
- ◆ changing spellings
- ◆ altering word order
- ◆ updating verb forms
- ◆ altering sentence lengths
- ◆ updating terms of reference, such as forms of address and dates.

COMPARISON TEXT

This text is a modern email. The influence of text messaging from mobile phones is seeping into email language and structure.

> Alright m8
> Not heard from u in ages. Wot u up to? Been busy revising 4 exams and glad that they are now over. Looking forward to summer hols. Dad plans to take us to Florida for 2 weeks to do Disneyland and generally chill. Sis wants to go to the water parks for a laugh and the olds fancy seeing the Kennedy Space Centre. Wot r your plans for the summer? Give me a call if u wanna meet up and do sumfing. We could go to the flicks or have a kick about in the park. Would be good to catch up after last few months.
> Cheers
> Ben

ACTIVITY Compare the email with Margaret Paston's letter. Look at:

- ◆ structure (use of paragraphs)
- ◆ level of formality
- ◆ language that is new or no longer used
- ◆ sentence lengths and types
- ◆ spellings
- ◆ openings and endings.

FURTHER READING

John Ayto, *Oxford School Dictionary of Word Origins* (OUP, 2002)
Bill Bryson, *Mother Tongue: The English Language* (Penguin, 1991)
Geoffrey Chaucer *The Canterbury Tales* (Oxford World's Classics, OUP, 1998). This is a translation into modern English by David Wright.
Geoffrey Chaucer, *The Riverside Chaucer Third Edition* (OUP, 1988)
The Paston Letters - A Selection in Modern Spelling, (Oxford World's Classics, OUP, 1999)
Oxford Student's Dictionary (Ed Robert Allen, OUP 2002). This dictionary contains some word origins.

3: Texts as products of an age

Introduction

Texts are products of the time in which they are written. They reflect ideas and beliefs common to that period. During the Elizabethan and Jacobean periods, time was a popular theme for writers. Through the concept of time, writers explored human mortality and people's place in the world as well as reinforcing current beliefs, especially religious ones. This unit explores texts from the Renaissance period focusing on the theme of time (the Renaissance, meaning 'rebirth', was the period in Europe from the early 1300s to the late sixteenth century during which classical ideals and artistic styles were revived).

CORE TEXTS

Poem 1
Untitled by A.W.
(The poet has never been identified)

Eternal time, that wastest without waste,
That art and art not, diest and livest still;
Most slow of all and yet of greatest haste;
Both ill and good, and neither good nor ill;
   How can I justly praise thee or dispraise?
   Dark are thy nights, but bright and clear thy days.

Both free and scarce, thou giv'st and tak'st again;
Thy womb, that all doth breed, is tomb to all;
Whatso by thee hath life, by thee is slain;
From thee do all things rise, by thee they fall;
   Constant, inconstant, moving, standing still;
   Was, Is, Shall be, do thee both breed and kill.

I lose thee while I seek to find thee out;
The farther off, the more I follow thee;
The faster hold, the greater cause of doubt;
Was, Is, I know; but Shall I cannot see.
   All things by thee are measured; thou, by none;
   All are in thee; thou, in thyself alone.

Poem 2
Sonnet XII
by William Shakespeare

When I do count the clock that tells the time,
And see the brave day sunk in hideous night;
When I behold the violet past prime,
And sable curls, all silvered o'er with white;
When lofty trees I see barren of leaves,
Which erst from heat did canopy the herd,
And summer's green all girded up in sheaves,
Borne on the bier with white and bristly beard:
Then of thy beauty do I question make,
That thou among the wastes of time must go,
Since sweets and beauties do themselves forsake
And die as fast as they see others grow,
    And nothing 'gainst Time's scythe can make defence
    Save breed, to brave him when he takes thee hence.

Poem 3
To The Virgins, To Make Much of Time
by Robert Herrick

Gather ye rosebuds while ye may,
Old Time is still a-flying:
And this same flower that smiles to-day,
To-morrow will be dying.

The glorious lamp of heaven, the sun,
The higher he's a-getting,
The sooner will his race be run,
And nearer he's to setting.

That age is best which is the first,
When youth and blood are warmer;
But being spent, the worse, and worst
Times still succeed the former.

Then be not coy, but use your time,
And while ye may, go marry;
For having lost but once your prime,
You may for ever tarry.

Getting started

ACTIVITIES 1 Read poem 1 by A.W. The poet uses antithesis (contrast) when talking about time. Find a few examples of this and explain what effect you think he wanted to create.

2 Renaissance poets were skilled at using different poetic forms. Copy and complete the grid below, exploring the form of each poem.

	Poem 1	Poem 2	Poem 3
Rhyme scheme			
Stanza structure			
Metre (See page 90)			

Development

ACTIVITIES 3 There are patterns in rhyme scheme, stanza structure and metre in each poem. Suggest reasons why each poem is structured in the way that it is. Is there any connection between the form and content? For example, why might longer lines be more suitable for poem 1 than for poem 3? Which poems use rhyming couplets and to what effect?

4 Look back at question 1. The poet used antithesis when talking about time. Re-read the Shakespeare sonnet and find examples of antithesis. How effective do you think they are?

5. How do Shakespeare and Herrick suggest we combat our destruction by time? Hint – look at the end of each poem.

Extension

ACTIVITIES 6 Renaissance poets used elaborate description and poetic techniques to discuss their subjects. Copy the grid below and complete it.

Example	Technique	Effect created
And this same flower that smiles to-day,/To-morrow will be dying (Herrick)		
And see the brave day sunk in hideous night (Shakespeare)		
The glorious lamp of heaven, the sun (Herrick)		
Thy womb, that all doth breed, is tomb to all (A.W.)		
And nothing 'gainst Time's scythe can make defence (Shakespeare)		

7 All three poems have several similarities in their approach to the theme of time. Explore what connections you can see between the poems. Use your answers to all the questions to help you, especially those from question 6.

ADDITIONAL STUDY

ACTIVITY People often say that we live in a fast-paced world where we expect everything to be completed quickly. Think about how developments in technology, transport and communications enable us to do things quickly. How might the theme of time be explored today? Write your own poem focusing on time.

Think about:

◆ form (will it be an established one or free verse?)
◆ rhyme scheme (will it have one?)
◆ language – it will need to reflect modern life – you could include mobile phone text language and email language
◆ content – think about the pressure on and value of our time today.

Once you have written your poem, present it to your class and be prepared to explain why you wrote it in the way that you did. Your teacher might use this to assess your speaking and listening for GCSE English.

COMPARISON TEXT

ACTIVITY Many themes run throughout literature such as:

◆ power ◆ love ◆ death
◆ money, wealth and social position ◆ weather.

Select a theme and find two or three texts that focus on it. You might choose to use poetry, prose, drama or non-fiction. Ensure that these texts relate to the same period (or if you are feeling really ambitious, look at the theme across time). Think about using the library, the internet (do a websearch for e-texts – electronic texts that you can then cut and paste), anthologies and newspapers.

Once you have selected a few texts, analyze how the theme has been presented. Look at:

◆ form and structure   ◆ content   ◆ use of language
◆ different approaches to the theme.

FURTHER READING

The Oxford Book of Sixteenth Century Verse ed. Emrys Jones (OUP, 2002)
The Oxford Book of Seventeenth Century Verse ed. Alistair Fowler (OUP, 2002)
The Oxford Book of the Sea ed. Jonathan Raban (OUP, 2001)
The Faber Book of Beasts ed. Paul Muldoon (Faber, 1997)
The Faber Book of London ed. A. N. Wilson (Faber, 1994)

1: Semantics

Semantics is the branch of linguistics (the science of language) that deals with the meaning of words and sentences. One aspect of semantics is the relationship between word meanings, for example the relationship between synonyms and antonyms.

Synonym

A synonym is a word that has a similar meaning to another word in the same language. For example, *happy*, *merry* and *jolly* are all synonyms, although they all have slightly different connotations.

Antonym

An antonym is a word opposite in meaning to another word in the same language, e.g. *bad* is the antonym of *good*; *happy* is the antonym of *sad*.

Shakespeare sometimes played with antonyms in his language. In the following quotations, identify the antonyms. How is Shakespeare twisting them? Can you see how he is undermining them by the implication that they are not in fact opposites, but very similar or closely allied?

Fair is foul, and foul is fair
Macbeth Act 1 Scene 1

My grave is like to be my wedding bed
Romeo and Juliet Act 1 Scene 5

My only love sprung from my only hate
Romeo and Juliet Act 1 Scene 5

Cannot be ill, cannot be good
Macbeth Act 1 Scene 3

Shakespeare often used synonyms and antonyms to create tension and startling images in his plays.

> Here's much to do with hate, but more with love:
> Why then, O brawling love, O loving hate,
> O any thing of nothing first create!
> O heavy lightness, serious vanity,
> Misshapen chaos of well-seeming forms,
> Feather of lead, bright smoke, cold fire, sick health,
> Still-waking sleep, that is not what it is!

Romeo and Juliet Act 1 Scene 1

In this extract, synonyms and antonyms are used to create the tension of the situation in Romeo's mood. He uses oxymoron (juxtaposing terms which seem contradictory). For example *cold fire* is a startling image because we usually associate heat and warmth with fire, not cold. How many other examples of oxymoron can you identify in this extract?

2: PHONOLOGY

Phonology is the study of sounds in a language. We can use words to create sound effects in a variety of ways. For example, we can use language to develop rhythm or give momentum to a text. Read the extract below and consider how the poet is using the sounds of the words.

> This is the Night Mail crossing the Border,
> Bringing the cheque and the postal order,
> Letters for the rich, letters for the poor,
> The shop at the corner, the girl next door.

From 'Night Mail' by W.H. Auden

Auden uses a wide range of sound patterning here:

This *is* (assonance)
Thi*s is* ... *cro*ssing (alliteration)
Br*i*ng*i*ng (assonance)
Letters for the ... letters for the (repetition)
The ... the (repetition).

Auden also uses rhythm to create the sound of the night mail train. Notice how in the first line the pace is steady but then accelerates in the second and third lines (as there are more unstressed syllables together) and slows down in the last line. The metre is very carefully controlled here; / marks a stressed syllable and ∪ an unstressed one. The vertical line shows how the rhythm is created by controlled units (feet):

/ ∪ ∪ / ∪ / ∪ ∪ / ∪
This is the / Night Mail / crossing the / Border,

/ ∪ ∪ / ∪ ∪ / ∪ / ∪
Bringing the / cheque and the / postal / order,

/ ∪ ∪ ∪ / / ∪ ∪ ∪ /
Letters / for the rich, / letters / for the poor,

∪ / ∪ ∪ / ∪ ∪ / ∪ /
The shop at / the corner, / the girl / next door.

Each line has four stressed syllables, but the pace of the train is created by the variety in the feet. Notice also how Auden is writing in the main tradition of English poetry by using ten syllables in each line.

Metre

Metre is a rhythmical pattern in verse, constructed with a combination of stressed and unstressed beats. You can see this in the above example, which contains most of the feet commonly used in the main tradition of English poetry:

iamb ∪ /
trochee / ∪
dactyl / ∪∪
anapaest ∪∪ /
amphibrach ∪ / ∪

Scansion

Scansion is the analysis of the pattern of the metre.

Rhyme

Rhyme is the matching of sounds at the end of words. It is often used in poetry, where the final word of one line rhymes with the final word of another line or lines (not necessarily consecutive lines). In the above extract, Auden uses the rhyme scheme *aa, bb*.

Vowel sounds

Against the rubber tongues of cows and the hoeing hands of men
Thistles spike the summer air
Or crackle open under a blue-black pressure

From 'Thistles' by Ted Hughes

The letters that make up the vowel sounds are: *a, e, i, o* and *u*.
Although these five letters are the recognized vowels in writing, there
are more than 20 vowel sounds that we pronounce in English. The use
of these vowel sounds differs greatly between different accents. In the
extract above, Hughes uses words that contain harsh vowel sounds, to
add to the atmosphere. For example, the *a* in *crackle* is a short, hard
sound, reinforcing the sense of power. The *i* in *thistles* is the short
vowel form, to reflect the aggressive nature of the thistles.

Assonance

> A dirtier sleetier snow, blow smokily unendingly, over

From 'Tractor' by Ted Hughes

Assonance is the recurrent use of the same or similar vowel sounds to
create special effects. Look at how Hughes creates the confusion of the
scene (created by the snow and wind) by using assonance in *dirtier
sleetier* and *snow, blow, smokily . . . over*. Whereas rhyme creates harmony,
rhythm and momentum, assonance here creates an unharmonious feel
and suggests the confusion and irregular nature of the scene.

Consonance

> The wind flung a magpie away and a black-
> Back gull bent like an iron bar slowly

From 'Wind' by Ted Hughes

Consonance is the repetition of sounds in the same position in a
sequence of words.

In this extract, Hughes uses consonance in *black-back*, which slows the
scene down and reinforces the difficulty that the bird experiences in
flying. This is later echoed in *slowly*.

3: WORD CLASS AND MORPHOLOGY

Word classes (also known as 'parts of speech') are the sets of words
that perform the same function in sentences, e.g. nouns, verbs,
adjectives, etc. This section revises word classes, but remember that
words can belong to different word classes in different contexts. For
example, in one sentence a word might be a verb, e.g. *I **cook** Sunday
lunch each week.* Here, *cook* is a verb. In another sentence, *cook* could be
used as a noun, e.g. *The **cook** is preparing school lunch.*

Morphology is the study of the structure of words. This includes looking at how word endings change (inflections). For example, we use inflections to express different verb tenses, e.g. *-ed*, *-ing*; the singular and plural of nouns; and the comparative and superlative forms of adjectives, e.g. *-er*, *-est*.

When studying morphology, words are broken down into their smallest elements (morphemes). Some words cannot be broken down into smaller grammatical parts, e.g. *boy*, but others can be broken down into prefixes and suffixes, which link on to the main root (or 'base') words. For example, *disgracefully*, can be broken down into the root word *-grace-*, the prefix *dis-* and the suffix *-fully*.

As you revise word classes, consider individual words and try to identify morphemes within them.

Noun
Nouns name things. They fall into several categories:

1 Noun – typical name of something, e.g. *house*; *television*
2 Proper noun – a name used for an individual person, place, animal, country, title, etc. and spelt with a capital letter, e.g. *David Beckham*; *Sheffield*; *America*
3 Collective noun – denotes a group, e.g. *army*; *government*
4 Abstract noun – noun that lacks physical reference, e.g. *success*; *failure*
5 Noun phrase – a series of adjectives built around a noun, e.g. *a small country dwelling*
6 Singular only nouns – never written in any other form, e.g. *homework*; *physics*
7 Plural only nouns – often names of two-part items, e.g. *binoculars*; *scissors*

Adjective
An adjective is a word which describes or relates to a noun.
1 Typically, an adjective comes before a noun to describe it, e.g. *the triumphant victory*; *a vicious dog*.
2 An adjective can stand alone after a verb, e.g. *The car was rusty*.
3 An adjective can be preceded by an intensifier, e.g. *a **very** violent creature*.
4 An adjective has different forms, e.g. the comparative and superlative (**bigger** and **biggest**).

Verb

A verb is a word used to indicate an action, state, or occurrence.

1 A sentence might contain a single verb, e.g. *The sun shone brightly down on us.*

2 It might contain one or more auxiliary verb (an auxiliary verb is used in forming the tenses, moods and voices of other verbs). For example, *They **must** come; They **must have** come; They **must have been** coming.*

3 Modal verbs – these are a type of auxiliary verb, which add precision to the verbs and suggest the likelihood of events. For example '*can*'; '*could*'; '*may*'; '*might*'; '*will*'; '*would*'; '*shall*'; '*should*'; '*must*'; '*dare*'; '*need*'; '*ought to*'; '*used to*'

4 Verb tense – where the verb indicates the time that it is taking place.
   ◆ Present tense – *I watch TV*, or present continuous *I am watching TV.*
   ◆ Past tense – *I watched TV* (completed action) or habitual one *I used to watch TV* or *I was watching TV.*
   ◆ Future tense – *I will/shall watch TV.*
   ◆ Conditional tense – suggesting some element of doubt *I could watch TV* or *I might watch TV* or *I would like to watch TV.*
   ◆ Future perfect tense – *I will/shall have watched TV.*
   ◆ Pluperfect tense – shows an action completed prior to some past point of time, e.g. *I had watched TV.*

5 Infinitive – the form of the verb expressing the verbal notion without subject or tense. For example, *to go*; *to see*; *to sing*

Adverb

An adverb refers back to a verb and describes how the verb is being performed.

1 Most adverbs are formed by adding *-ly* to an adjective, e.g. *quick – quickly*; *slow – slowly*. Remember that some adverbs alter their spelling slightly when adding the suffix *–ly*, e.g. *happy – happily.*

2 Adverbial phrases add more information to a sentence. They tell us manner (how), time (when), or place (where), something is done. They can be used in various positions in a sentence but most frequently come at the end. For example:

   a *I came to school **by bus*** (manner)
   b ***At ten o'clock** the plane departed for New York* (time)
   c *I arranged to meet her **outside the park*** (place)
   They can also be used to link clauses together. For example:
   ◆ *The train was full. **However**, I managed to find a seat.*
   ◆ ***Frankly**, I am unhappy with the situation.*

Pronoun

Pronouns stand in place of nouns.

1 Personal pronouns identify speakers, e.g. *I*; *you*; *he*; *she*; *it*; *we*; *they*.
2 Reflexive pronouns can be used in two ways:
   ◆ for a direct or indirect object that refers to the same person or thing as the subject of the clause, e.g. *They didn't wash **themselves***
   ◆ for emphasis, e.g. *He said to **himself***.
3 Possessive pronouns express ownership, e.g. *my*; *mine*; *your*; *yours*.
4 Relative pronouns are used to link a subordinate clause to the head of a noun phrase, e.g. *That's the boy **who** caused the trouble.* Other relative pronouns include: *whom*; *which*; *that*.
5 Demonstrative pronouns express a contrast, e.g. *Have **this** one here, not **that** one there.*

Preposition

Prepositions are items that govern and precede (come before) nouns and pronouns, e.g. *in*; *to*; *by*; *under*; *over*; *after*; *between*. For example, *The box is **under** the bed **by** the door.*

Connective or conjunction

These join clauses or ideas together and fall into several categories:

1 those which show addition or sequence, e.g. *and*
2 those which show contrast, e.g. *but*
3 those which show alternatives, e.g. *or*
4 pairs which work together, e.g. *either . . . or*; *neither . . . nor*
5 those which link units of meaning or clauses in a sentence that might not otherwise stand together:
   ◆ time – *until*; *when*, e.g. *I stayed **until** it got dark*
   ◆ place - *where*, e.g. *I think I know **where** you are*
   ◆ condition – *if*, e.g. *I will call **if** he does not arrive by six*
   ◆ concession – *though*, e.g. *I like her music, **though** the last song was poor*
   ◆ purpose – *in order to*, e.g. *He went to Spain **in order to** see his family*
   ◆ reason – *because*, e.g. *I can't come **because** I'm ill.*

Determiner

A determiner is an item that links with a noun to express number or quantity, e.g. *a*; *the*; *every*.

4: SYNTAX

The term 'syntax' describes the arrangement of words and phrases in a sentence. Writers (and speakers) manipulate sentences to create specific effects, for example to control the pace of a narrative, to build and reduce the tension, and to add dramatic effects.

Read the following extract in which the author uses many different sentence structures to create different effects.

Discourse connective

Compound sentence

Complex sentence: first part main clause: second part subordinate clause

Simple sentence

For an hour we followed the gorillas at a near trot through the bamboo. Most of the time we could not see them, but we could hear them crashing through the underbrush. Sometimes they were very close, but we were never able to see them well.

Finally the gorillas stopped for their midday rest. The big male rolled over on his back and lazily chomped bamboo. He was perhaps ten yards away. I was frustrated: I wanted to take his picture, but he was low in the brush. For a while, all we saw was a huge hand rising up, grabbing the bamboo, and descending again out of sight. Occasionally he would raise his massive head, look at us, and then lie back again. I busied myself with cameras and lenses, trying to get ready for a coming opportunity to film him. Changing lenses, adjusting f-stop . . .

What happened next was extraordinarily fast. There was a deafening roar, a sound as loud as a subway train rushing into a station. I looked up to see the huge male charging directly at me. He was moving incredibly swiftly, bellowing with rage. He was coming right at me.

I moaned and ducked down, pushing my face into the underbrush, backing off. A strong arm gripped my shirt at the shoulders. This is it. There had been cases where the gorillas attacked people. Picked them up and bit them and threw them around like a dishrag. Months in the hospital. Now the gorilla was grabbing me . . .

From *Travels* by Michael Crichton

Simple sentence

A simple sentence contains one clause (i.e. a subject and a verb which says something about that subject. Simple sentences allow the writer to build the tension and create an arresting effect for the reader. In a text for a young reader, they are used to convey basic information.

Compound sentence

A compound sentence contains one or more ideas linked by a connective such as *and*, *but*, or *or*. Compound sentences enable the writer to add detail and build up the scene.

Complex sentence

A complex sentence contains a main clause that can stand on its own, and a subordinate clause, which cannot stand on its own. Complex sentences can build detail and pack more information into the text. They can also enable the writer to add drama to a scene.

Discourse connectives

Discourse connectives signal the stages of the scene and add chronology.